BUDGET
SCRAPBOOKING

Great ideas for scrapbooking on a shoestring

MEMORY
MAKERS
BOOKS

Executive Editor Kerry Arquette

Founder Michele Gerbrandt

Editors MaryJo Regier, Lydia Rueger

Art Director Nick Nyffeler

Designers Andrea Zocchi, Robin Rozum

Art Acquisitions Editor Janetta Abucejo Wieneke

Craft Editor Jodi Amidei

Photographer Ken Trujillo

Contributing Photographers Christina Dooley, Brenda Martinez, Jennifer Reeves

Contributing Writers Julie Labuzsewski, MaryJo Regier, Lydia Rueger

Contributing Memory Makers Masters Valerie Barton, Joanna Bolick, Susan Cyrus, Lisa Dixon, Kathy Fesmire, Diana Graham, Diana Hudson, Kelli Noto, Michelle Pesce, Shannon Taylor, Denise Tucker, Andrea Lyn Vetten-Marley, Holle Wiktorek

Editorial Support Karen Cain, Emily Curry Hitchingham, Dena Twinem

Memory Makers® Budget Scrapbooking

Published by Memory Makers Books, an imprint of F+W Publications, Inc.

12365 Huron Street, Suite 500, Denver, CO 80234

Phone 1-800-254-9124

First edition. Printed in China.

08 07 06 05 04 5 4 3 2 1

Library of Congress Cataloging-in-Publication Data

Budget scrapbooking : great ideas for scrapbooking on a shoestring.
    p. cm.
    Includes bibliographical references.
    ISBN 1-892127-44-X
    1. Photograph albums. 2. Photographs–Conservation and restoration. 3. Scrapbooks. 4. Found objects (Art)

TR465.B83 2004
745.593–dc22

2004059295

Distributed to trade and art markets by

F+W Publications, Inc.

4700 East Galbraith Road, Cincinnati, OH 45236

Phone 1-800-289-0963

ISBN 1-892127-44-X

Memory Makers Books is the home of *Memory Makers*, the scrapbook magazine dedicated to educating and inspiring scrapbookers. To subscribe, or for more information, call 1-800-366-6465.
Visit us on the Internet at www.memorymakersmagazine.com

THIS BOOK
BELONGS TO

Dedicated to collectors of found objects, pack rats and garage sale connoisseurs everywhere. May the items you've accumulated over the years find new life as scrapbook page embellishments.

Table of Contents

CHAPTER 1:
Kitchen 12-27

Accent pages with product labels, produce bags, aluminum foil, plastic utensils, bottle caps, coffee filters and more.

CHAPTER 2:
Bed & Bath 28-47

Combine your memories with vintage jewelry, scraps of clothing, potpourri, cotton balls, children's toys and other fun items.

CHAPTER 3:
Home Office 48-63

Complement photos using a variety of home-office supplies, including paper clips, file folders, cork board, filmstrips, CDs, self-stick notes and staples.

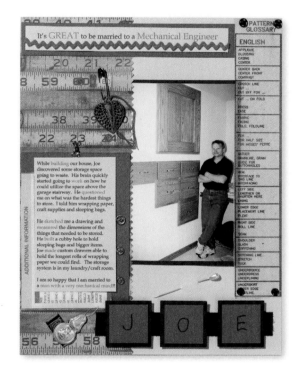

CHAPTER 4:
Craft Room 64-79

Embellish scrapbooks with items commonly used for sewing and other crafts, such as ribbon, feathers, felt, fringe, clay and rickrack.

CHAPTER 5:
Garage & Workshop 80-93

Conjure up page themes as you sort through old tools, license plates, fishing lures, screen mesh, washers and more.

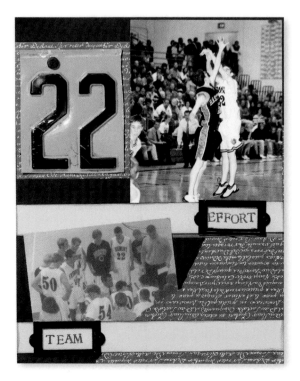

Gerbrandts

There is a truth, in that old saying
that one man's trash is another's' gaining.
If you take the time, you too will see
treasures all around, just waiting for thee

The bits and pieces of our family's lives
are often sitting right in front of our eyes.
A new perspective is all one needs
to create precious flowers from apparent weeds.

For happiness is all around
in every room, is where it's found.
Wherever our family happens to be
is where you'll find true joys key.

written by Torrey Miller

Introduction

Against the white cabinets and light-colored walls of my kitchen sits a cobalt blue enamel canister set. Its brilliant color is a dramatic contrast to the neutral backdrop, and I love the fact that the largest canister can hold an entire bag of flour. The canisters have been the focal point of my kitchen for the past 10 years—not bad for something I bought for $10 at a flea market!

Searching for bargains and slightly used treasures is a family affair at my house. When my kids were younger, they had so many secondhand items that they didn't know clothing came with tags! Today, on certain Saturdays, my oldest daughter and I take off to garage sales on bikes with $20 in our pockets and a few empty bags. Our motto is "Buy whatever we can carry home while staying within our $20 budget."

If you're a seeker and collector of found objects like me, you'll love *Budget Scrapbooking*. You won't believe the items scrapbook artists found to enhance their pages by hunting through the rooms of their homes. They cut snowflakes from coffee filters, wove dental floss around page borders and more to prove that anything goes in scrapbooking—anything, that is, except the money in your bank account.

Browse through the following pages featuring found objects from the kitchen, bedroom, bathroom, home office, craft room and garage to discover how old and forgotten items become new again on scrapbook pages. Then, shuffle through the drawers and closets at your house to discover some one-of-a-kind page accents of your own. The flea market mentality can help as you hunt—always keep an open mind and look for beauty in the most unlikely places.

Michele

Michele Gerbrandt

Founding Editor

Memory Makers magazine

Getting Started

Five years ago, if you asked a scrapbooker where she keeps her metal eyelets or brads, she probably would have laughed at you. Today, eyelets and brads are as common as cardstock in many scrapbookers' workspaces, and that's just the beginning. It seems almost anything goes when it comes to embellishing pages. If you're concerned about safety and preservation, you can still incorporate found items on pages by keeping them away from photos, de-acidifying them with a spray or encasing them in PVC-free memorabilia pockets. For additional protection, always use duplicate photos when working with questionable supplies. With that in mind, even small objects found around your house can become page accents. And not only will scrapbooking with found objects allow you to create pages that are truly one-of-a-kind, they'll save you money, too!

Found Item Scavenger Hunt

The challenge to using found objects on pages is that they are not conveniently sorted and labeled next to papers and stickers in your scrapbook workspace. These items are tucked in the backs of closets and cupboards, covered by other items in drawers and stashed in the garage. Have your own scavenger hunt around the house before you crop to help you locate and organize items that would work well as page embellishments.

Begin by gathering clear plastic storage bags for every room in the house—bedroom, bathroom, kitchen, home office, sewing/hobby room and garage or workshop. Label each bag with a room name. Moving from room to room, search for items that might lend themselves to scrapbook pages and place those items in the corresponding bag. Assign certain rooms to willing family members to make the hunting process go more quickly. Trinkets from your jewelry box that you may have considered throwing out will suddenly take on new meaning. Packaging and labels from the kitchen may never see the bottom of the plastic recycling bin again.

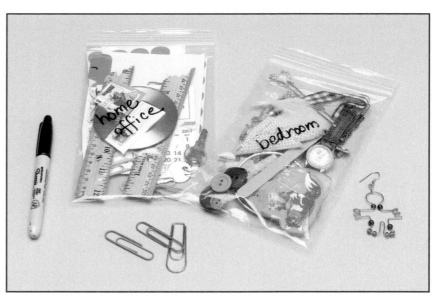

By the time you reach the second room, an interesting and magical phenomenon takes place: Your brain begins to automatically catalog certain found items that would coordinate well with your photos. Perhaps an old brooch would be perfect for a heritage page, or a mesh bag used to hold tomatoes would work well with shoreline photos.

Keep the items in bags near your scrapbook supplies to sort through when looking for that perfect embellishment. Refer to the checklists at the beginning of each chapter to help you identify possible page embellishments from each room.

Hosting a Found Object Swap

One woman's trash really does become another woman's treasure when you host a Found Object Swap. Ask each guest to bring a bag filled with items found around her house. When guests arrive, place their bags on a table, survey the assortment of treasures and begin swapping! Before you send out invitations, take time to define the logistics of the swap (suggestions listed below). Ask a friend for suggestions or search for "scrapbook swaps" online for information. The site, www.suite101.com/welcome.cfm/scrapbooking, contains an extensive list of points to consider before hosting swaps in general. In addition, the following suggestions will help you in planning.

• Remember that it might be impossible for a found item swap to function like a traditional supply swap in which every participant ends up with an identical set of items. Make sure this is clear to swap participants before they sign up.

• Decide if you'd like the swap to take place in your home or online. For online swaps, Yahoo Groups (www.groups.yahoo .com) is a great place to spread the word about your swap if you aren't already part of an online community.

• Ask participants to organize items by type (buttons, jewelry, fabric, product labels, etc.) or by the rooms in which the items were found. You may consider limiting the hunt to one designated room of the house or even to one type of object. Copy the "Found Item Scavenger Hunt" information shown on page 8 to familiarize everyone with the concept.

• Determine if there should be limits on size, weight and thickness of found items so the objects contributed will be feasible to use on scrapbook pages.

• Consider a catchy, intriguing title to generate interest in your swap, such as "Forgotten Finds," "Trash to Treasure" or "Anything Goes."

• Brainstorm themes that might work well with found objects and incorporate that theme into your invitation style and décor. For example, play on the idea of found "treasures" with a pirate theme.

• Would you like to make your event a crop-n-swap? If cropping time will follow the swap, remember to tell guests to bring photos and scrapbook supplies.

• After swapping time is completed, offer an incentive for scrapbookers to create pages out of what they've found. Give a prize to the first person to complete a page with a newly acquired found object.

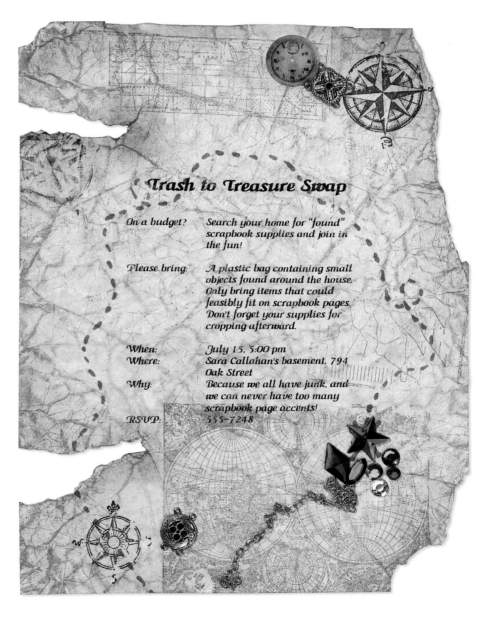

Trash to Treasure Swap

On a budget? Search your home for "found" scrapbook supplies and join in the fun!

Please bring: A plastic bag containing small objects found around the house. Only bring items that could feasibly fit on scrapbook pages. Don't forget your supplies for cropping afterward.

When: July 15, 5:00 pm
Where: Sara Callahan's basement, 794 Oak Street
Why: Because we all have junk, and we can never have too many scrapbook page accents!
RSVP: 555-7248

Found Finds

If you can't find scrapbook-worthy objects in your house, flea markets, yard sales and thrift stores are great resources for cheap and sometimes free page accents. Below are some items that our scrapbook artists have purchased for next to nothing. Some they've used on pages "as is," while others they've altered, cut or pulled apart to suit their needs. Be on the lookout for:

Baby clothing

Bag of sand and sea shells

Beads

Belt buckles

Bib overalls

Birth annoucements

Board games

Books

Bracelets

Broken items found at the bottom of flea-market bins

Buttons

Calligraphy pen tips

Ceramic tiles

Clothing with embroidery

Dictionaries

Doll house furniture

Dominoes

Dress patterns

Earrings

Fabric/cloth

Game pieces

Game score cards

Greeting cards

Hair accessories

Handkerchiefs with embroidery

Hook-and-eye fasteners

Invitations

Lace

Lapel pins and buttons

Library pockets

Maps

Necklaces

Needle and thread

Playing cards

Postage stamps

Puzzle pieces

Ribbons

Rickrack

Scrabble tiles

Seam binding tape

Stationery

Travel brochures

Watch parts

Yarn

Zippers

Andrea Lyn Vetten-Marley of Aurora, Colorado, is a self-proclaimed "junk-hoarder" and shops extensively at yard sales and thrift stores in search of scrapbook page embellishments. She purchased 15 yards of heirloom lace for 50 cents, some of which was used for a border on this spread. Hook-and-eye fasteners, purchased for 10 cents, also accent this page. In addition, Andrea says she has spread the word to her friends that she is always on the lookout for such items. "People give me loads of free stuff that they want to get rid of," she says. "I pick through what I can use and pass the rest on!"

Online Freebies

The Internet is full of resources for scrapbookers on a budget. Check out the following Web sites or do a search for "scrapbooking + free" to see what comes up. In addition, many scrapbook shopping sites offer free gifts for purchasing certain quantities or include links to other freebies.

MULTIPLE FREE OFFERINGS

These sites include links to free scrapbooking items and information all over the Internet, including printable page accents, patterns, layout inspiration, genealogy charts, articles and much more.

www.scrapbooking.about.com/od/freestuff

www.craftfreebies.com/scrapbooks.html

www.100megsfree3.com/arlana/freebies/crafts.htm

www.FreebieDot.com/40p1.htm

www.allfreecrafts.com/craftlinks.htm

www.bellaonline.com/subjects/3279.asp

www.scrapbooksites.com/links.asp?cat=3p

www.misterinkjet.com/printable-scrapbooking-links.htm

COMPUTER FONTS

www.1001fonts.com

www.fontgarden.com

www.larabiefonts.com/index.html

www.dafont.com/en

www.onescrappysite.com

www.fontface.com

www.fontconnection.com

CLIP ART

www.best-of-clipart.com

www.free-clipart.net

www.free-clip-art.com

www.clip-art.easy-interactive.com

www.cutecolors.com

Printable page accents from Prim Graphics and Lyndsay's Scrapping Place are just a few examples of free printable page accents found online.

PAPER-PIECING PATTERNS

www.scrapbooking.about.com/cs/freepatterns/index.htm?once=true&

www.patternpage.com/freepatterns.htm

www.scrapjazz.com/links/Inspiration/paper_piecings

www.scraplink.com/pp.htm

www.collectedmemories.com/cgi-bin/WebObjects/cmStore.woa/wa/page?key=freediecuts

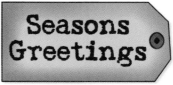

PRINTABLE PAGE ACCENTS AND DESIGNS

www.scrapping-place.com/freebies.html

www.gulf-shores-alabama-condo-rentals.com/beach-scrapbook-printables.html

ww.primgraphics.com/freetags.htm

www.disney.go.com/magicartist/index_main.html

www.thelittlepillow.com/albumpgdl.html

www.raggedyscrappin.com/store/piclink.asp?pageID=FreeGraphics

www.primdoodles.com/printables.asp

C H A P T E R 1

Kitchen

The kitchen is the essential hub of most households. It's estimated that today's wife and mother spends an average of 30 percent of her waking hours in the kitchen. Whether it's packing school lunches, restocking the pantry, baking homemade treats, preparing a meal, cleaning up afterward, talking on the phone or updating the calendar, time spent in the kitchen can yield a grocery bag of tiny treasures for your scrapbook pages.

While working and cleaning in your scullery, pay attention to the things you toss into the garbage pail. Bread-bag tabs, foil produce twist ties, favorite-food labels, juice lids, brown bags, cheesecloth and mesh fruit bags are among the many useful items that are easy to overlook. Plastic spoons and plates, foil, soda cans, Popsicle sticks, bottle caps and even drawer liners can be converted into clever scrapbook page accents. And don't forget about the tools you can make from items found in the kitchen: cookie cutters for shape templates, drinking straws for blowing paint and liquid dish soap for bubble painting.

It's easy to add handmade quality and artistic appeal to scrapbook pages from found kitchen items. So harvest those interesting culinary castoffs and use this chapter as inspiration for cooking up your own tasteful scrapbook pages!

Variety Is the Spice of Life

SEARCH YOUR KITCHEN FOR THESE GREAT FINDS

Anything goes when it comes to making hamburgers for the boys in the Regier household. MaryJo took the same approach when making her page using found objects from her kitchen. Flatten and adhere foil produce twist ties to page. Trim off excess paper from napkin and adhere to page. Encapsulate herbs with clear paper glaze. Adhere tag and twine from spice collection gift set. Place corner of photo in bread-bag tab. Attach sticker from tomato. Use colored lacquer for ketchup splat on journaling block.

MaryJo Regier, Memory Makers Books

Supplies Green floral patterned paper (Design Originals); red patterned paper (source unknown); red crystal lacquer (Sakura Hobby Craft); gold mulberry paper; clear paper glaze

Found Objects Paper napkin (Rafuse and Canadian Art Prints by House of Prill); foil produce twist ties; herbs; twine and tag from spice collection gift set; bread-bag tab; sticker from tomato

Found Treasures From the Kitchen

Birthday candles
Bottle caps
Bread-bag tabs
Broken plate/glass shards
Brown lunch sacks
Cheesecloth
Chopsticks
Cookbook pages
Cupcake papers
Decorative napkins
Drawer liners
Dried herbs

Egg dippers
Faux wax seals
Foil
Food labels
Juice and milk lids
Junk mail
Key rings
Menus
Mesh produce bags
Paper doilies
Paper plates
Paper towels

Plastic plates and silverware
Popsicle sticks
Produce stickers
Receipts
Recipe cards
Soda cans and tabs
String
Tiny matchboxes
Toothpicks
Wallpaper remnants

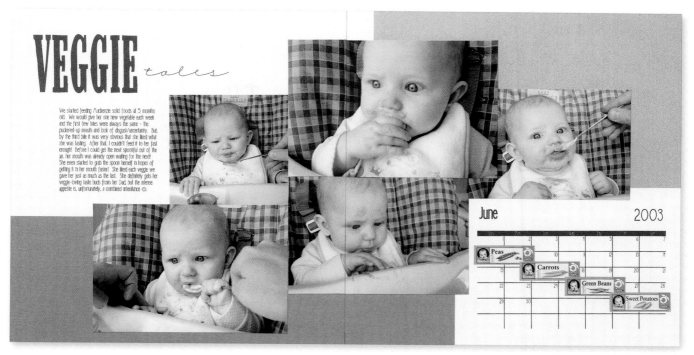

June 2003

Peas
Carrots
Green Beans
Sweet Potatoes

Veggie Tales

SAVE LABELS FROM BABY FOOD JARS

Heather documented when specific foods were introduced to her daughter using baby food jar labels and a simple calendar page. Use orange and green cardstock to match the colors of baby food labels. Adhere labels to a simple, computer-generated calendar or a page cut from an actual monthly calendar. Place baby food labels on calendar the week foods were introduced.

Heather Melzer, Yorkville, Illinois

Supplies Green, orange, white cardstocks; computer-generated calendar
Found Objects Labels from baby food jars

Grandma Mary Rueger would start preparing for the holidays months ahead by baking all types of cookies, including several Czech varieties, and then freezing them until Christmas. She would always read Christmas stories to my dad and his brothers. The boys' personalized matching shirts and stockings were gifts from Uncle Arnold Rueger, who worked at Sears.

Mary's Christmas

USE FOIL LIDS FROM MILK BOTTLES

To give her heritage page holiday ambiance, Lydia used green foil lids from delivered milk bottles. Make three circle shapes with circle punch. Journal on circle shape and adhere to center of lid. Attach foil lids to page. For tiny green circles, punch circles from another foil lid using small circle punch; place around page. Use green paper as page accent.

Lydia Rueger, Memory Makers Books

Supplies Title letters (QuickKutz); black, green and white cardstocks; circle punch
Found Objects Milk bottle lids

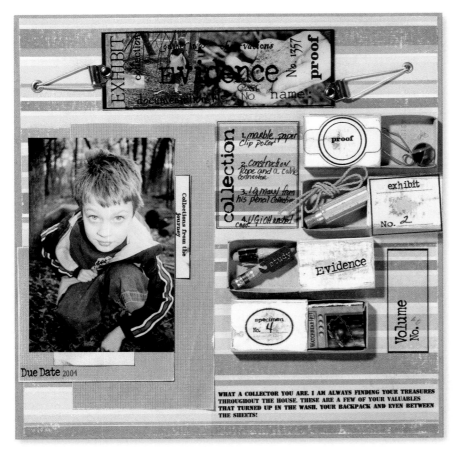

Evidence

DISPLAY COLLECTIBLES IN MATCHBOXES

Using four matchboxes, Diana show-cased the odds and ends her son collects. Use a sturdy chip board as a background. Sand patterned paper to give it a weathered look; mount on chip board. Print title on transparency and mount over cropped photo; adhere with eyelets, brackets, brads and elastic cord. Paint matchboxes with white acrylic paint using foam brush; dry with heat gun then sand to achieve weathered look. Mount matchboxes on page. Adhere transparencies to outside of matchboxes. Use a strong adhesive to adhere found objects to inside of match-boxes. Rub brown stamping ink on edges of journaling tab.

Diana Graham, Barrington, Illinois

Supplies Patterned paper (Chatterbox); clasps and elastic (7Gypsies); date stamp and study tag (Making Memories); white acrylic paint; brown stamping ink
Found Objects Chip board; matchboxes; transparencies; marble; clip poker; construction rope; cable connector; pencils; washed Yu-Gi-Oh! card

Cousins

JOURNAL ON A LUNCH BAG

Chris captured the innocence of childhood by journaling on a brown paper bag. To avoid a paper jam in the printer, print journaling on a plain piece of paper first, then position bag over text. Tape down edges of bag before running paper through the printer. Fold down top edge of bag; seal with wax seal. Mount bag on page. Repeat-edly stamp the word "family" on twill tape. Adhere tape to page.

Chris Douglas, East Rochester, Ohio

Supplies Patterned paper (Daisy D's); green cardstock; alphabet stamps (PSX Design); wax seal (Creative Imaginations); black stamping ink
Found Objects Brown paper bag; twill tape

Making Shapes

Trace around cookie cutters to make your own die cuts or cut your own shape template from a plastic coffee-can lid. Trace around cups, plates or a roll of tape to create circle shapes in any size.

H_2O

CREATE TEXTURE WITH COLORED CHEESECLOTH AND DOG BONE PACKAGING

To complement the mood of her beach photo, Michelle ingeniously created her own textured accents in muted colors. Adhere copper wire leaf and strip of brown plastic mesh from dog bone packaging to cardstock. Dye cheesecloth using a wet sponge soaked in walnut ink. Let dry. Wrap strip of cheesecloth around cardstock and tie on front side of layout. Create tassel with jute and shells. Accent page with wire twisted around small rocks. Use piece of cheesecloth and plastic mesh for title block. Place old vintage postcards in mini windows. Accent page corners with cheesecloth.

Michelle Miller, Fort Hood, Texas

Supplies Windowed cardstock (C-Thru Ruler); H_2O sticker (Creative Imaginations); lettering for title (EK Success); journaling block (Making Memories); walnut ink

Found Objects Cheesecloth; plastic mesh from dog bone packaging; copper wire leaf; label-maker labels; vintage postcards; seashells; jute; small rocks; wire

Chinese Take-Out

ADD ORIENTAL FLAIR WITH RESTAURANT ITEMS

Michelle captured her son's first experience eating Chinese food with an array of items from a Chinese restaurant. She even shaped a fortune cookie from clay to complete her layout. Make border by adhering rice to strong double-sided tape on cardstock. Dust tape with cornstarch to eliminate glare. Secure bamboo sushi mat to cardstock with stitches and adhesive. Tie red thread around chopsticks; adhere to page. Adhere paper parasol to page. Create mini album using take-out box as front cover. Tie household twine to mini album. Cut out letters for title. Adhere to rice paper. Adhere rice paper to sushi mat. Create fortune cookie using air-dry clay by adding tan paint to clay and shaping clay into fortune cookie shape. Let clay air dry then glaze. Rub chalk on edges to "brown" cookie. Cut off back of cookie to reduce bulk. Insert cookie into a fortune cookie bag with portion of paper fortune peeking out. Adhere to page.

Michelle Pendleton, Colorado Springs, Colorado

Supplies White rice paper (Club Scrap); air-dry clay (Provo Craft); tan cardstock; chalk; double-sided tape; glaze

Found Objects Uncooked rice; bamboo sushi mat; chopsticks; fortune cookie bag and paper fortune; paper parasol; take-out box from Chinese restaurant; household twine; cornstarch; acrylic paint

Christmas Fruit

ACCENT PAGE WITH A MESH FRUIT BAG

Ginger discovered the perfect textured embellishment for a page about a family who enjoys eating fruit: the bright red mesh bags they come in. Spread out fruit bag on page. Use brads to secure mesh bag to front of layout; use adhesive to secure mesh bag to back of layout. Use label from fruit bag and fruit charms as page accents.

Ginger McSwain, Cary, North Carolina

Supplies Gold patterned paper (Club Scrap)
Found Objects Mesh fruit bag and label; brads; charms

You Are Cordially Invited

SHOWCASE TEA-BAG PACKAGING

Using a white linen napkin, a formal invitation and colorful tea-bag packaging, Elizabeth conveyed that it's "teatime" on her page. Adhere napkin to patterned paper; fold excess around edges of paper and adhere to backside. Attach invitation. Use corner of tea-bag packaging as photo corners. Attach colorful tea-bag packages (ripped open and empty); dangle tea-bag tag from tea-bag package. Tie string and colorful tea-bag tags around side of photo. Adhere pocket for journaling tag. Make tassel for journaling tag using tea-bag tags. Attach empty sugar packets.

Elizabeth Ruuska, Rensselaer, Indiana

Supplies Yellow patterned paper (Mustard Moon)
Found Objects Linen napkin; invitation; tea-bag packages, tea-bag tags; pocket from tea-bag packaging; sugar packets; string

Instant Human

GATHER COFFEE PARAPHERNALIA

MaryJo cleverly captured her morning ritual on her layout using coffee beans, a stir stick and her own stamped coffee cup stains. To create coffee cup stains, ink bottom of coffee cup with brown ink and repeatedly stamp blue paper with coffee cup. Rub brown ink along edges of blue paper and mount on brown background paper. Adhere stamps from coffee bag to page. Use decorative scissors to make mats for mini photos of coffee bar. Adhere to page. Empty sugar packet and attach to page. Attach coffee beans and stained coffee stir stick. For tag, create background paper on computer using different fonts in various colors. Add glass slide over close-up photo. Punch hole on top of computer-generated tag; tie on brown ribbon.

MaryJo Regier, Memory Makers Books

Supplies Blue paper (Design Originals); green patterned paper (source unknown); brown cardstock; mulberry paper; brown stamping ink
Found Objects Coffee cup for stamp; coffee beans; sugar packet; stir stick; stamps from coffee-bean packaging; glass slide; brown ribbon

Lil' Aggies

TRANSFORM A PLASTIC SPOON

To convey team spirit on her layout, Summer made a football and page bubble using inexpensive plastic spoons. Cut off handles from two clear plastic spoons. Paint spoon to resemble a football. Adhere to page. Mount focal photo over rectangular piece of cheesecloth. Stitch embroidery floss on brown strips of paper to resemble stitching on football. Attach decorative strips to page. Adhere clear spoon over stamped date to create page bubble.

Summer Ford, San Antonio, Texas

Supplies: Plaid patterned paper (Lasting Impressions); rub-on title letters (Creative Imaginations); letter stamps (Hero Arts); burgundy cardstock; vellum

Found Objects Clear plastic spoons; cheesecloth; embroidery floss; eyelets

Frugal Bonus Idea #2

Adding Texture

Use sponges or crumpled plastic wrap dipped in paint to texturize cardstock for use as background paper, mats or tags. Or, sponge through a paper doily for a soft texture.

Christmas Wishes

FIND NEW USE FOR MESH FROM PIZZA BOX

Using found objects from her kitchen, Denise conveyed the spirit of the holidays on her page, complete with tinsel and snow. Cover a piece of cardstock with aluminum foil. Mount plastic mesh from pizza box on foil. Print title and journaling blocks on white paper; add adhesive to edges and immediately sprinkle salt on edges to create frost. Cut red mats and red accents from a red plastic plate.

Denise Tucker, Versailles, Indiana

Supplies Black cardstock; white paper
Found Objects Aluminum foil, plastic mesh from pizza box; red plastic plate; salt

Chocolate Sweet Tooth

HIDE JOURNALING BEHIND COCOA PACKAGING

To emphasize how much her daughter loves chocolate, Maureen featured the label from the baking cocoa container on her page. For background, use brown cardstock to resemble the color of chocolate. Attach strip of foil to page. Cut out front label from cocoa packaging. Attach to front of hidden-journaling panel; look inside to reveal journaling. Adhere journaling panel to page. Cut out back label featuring recipes from cocoa container and adhere to page.

Maureen Spell, Carlsbad, New Mexico

Supplies Black stickers (Creative Imaginations); red stickers and date stamp (Making Memories); brown cardstock; black stamping ink
Found Objects Front and back label from baking cocoa container; aluminum foil

Flying Lesson

FIND A NEW USE FOR RUG GRIPPER

When Paula saw a roll of rug gripper at the dollar store, she knew it would be a perfect and inexpensive way to add dimension to her vacation layout. Cut plastic gripper into strips. Adhere to page. Attach mat and photos over gripper. Use white feather and white brads to complement color of gripper. Consider using a piece of a rug gripper for goalie nets when making soccer and hockey layouts.

Paula Frances Jones, Caledon, Ontario, Canada

Supplies Blue and red cardstocks; transparency
Found Objects Plastic rug gripper; feather; brads

Summer Days

DECORATE PAGE WITH ALUMINUM CAN AND TABS

Chris captured "the real thing" with a flattened Coke can and tabs. Cut, wash and flatten out aluminum can. Use can as a background accent in layout. Adhere photo. Use tabs with brads in holes as picture holders. Use third tab as a buckle by threading ribbon through tab. Attach ribbon to strip of red paper and adhere to page.

Chris Douglas, East Rochester, Ohio

Supplies Silver patterned paper (KI Memories); rub-on letters (Making Memories); black and red cardstocks
Found Objects Soda can and tabs; ribbon; brads

Bubble-Painting Cardstock

Mix ¼-part dish soap with ¾-part water in a cup and add a few drops of food-coloring or bottled ink. Blow into mixture with a straw until bubble mound forms; lightly press cardstock facedown onto bubbles. Repeat as needed to cover cardstock; allow to dry.

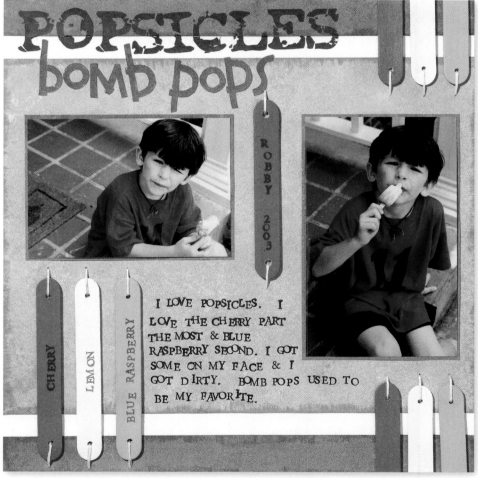

Popsicles Bomb Pops

USE POPSICLE STICKS AS A DESIGN ELEMENT

Shannon turned a simple summertime activity into a compelling page layout using painted Popsicle sticks. Punch holes through Popsicle sticks. Paint sticks with red, white and blue paint. Stamp words on sticks and attach to page using embroidery floss. For side embellishment, cut sticks in half and punch holes through ends. Line up half sticks on page and adhere with embroidery floss.

Shannon Taylor, Bristol, Tennessee

Supplies Patterned paper (Carolee's Creations); title stamps (Junque); journaling stamps (Hero Arts); white cardstock; stamping ink; chalk

Found Objects Popsicle sticks; embroidery floss; acrylic paint

Dyeing Eggs for Easter

EMBELLISH SEASONAL PAGE WITH EGG DIPPERS

Thinking ahead, Ruthann saved the wire egg dippers from the egg dyeing kit for an Easter layout. On left page, adhere egg dipper to page. On right page, make square vellum mat. Adhere egg dipper to mat. Journal on egg shape cut-out and slip into egg dipper. Use tinsel for grass in die-cut basket.

Ruthann Grabowski, Yorktown, Virginia

Supplies Yellow patterned paper (Doodlebug Design); green patterned paper (Provo Craft); vellum; egg stickers (Colorbök); die-cut basket; egg-shaped eyelets
Found Objects Wire egg dippers; tinsel

Hunter Is Four

LIVEN UP PAGE WITH BIRTHDAY DECORATIONS

Using candles, frosting letters, wrapping paper and other leftover party decorations, MaryJo captured her son's fourth birthday celebration on a dazzling and colorful layout. Create decorative border strips with wrapping paper. Attach crepe paper to center of border strips; twist crepe paper to create dimension. Adhere confetti to journaling block on tag. Tie gift ribbon to tag. Create oval mat for focal photo. Attach to page. Use frosting letters for title. Accent page with candles, shaker box from birthday card and green plastic "Happy Birthday" letters.

MaryJo Regier, Memory Makers Books

Supplies Light blue patterned paper (Karen Foster Design); stamps (Making Memories, Stampendous); yellow plaid patterned paper
Found Objects Birthday candles; confetti, crepe paper; ribbon; wrapping paper; shaker box cut from a birthday card; frosting letters; green plastic letters from flower bouquet

Baby Face

TRANSFORM BREAD-BAG TABS INTO DECORATIVE BEADS

Mendy found a new use for bread-bag tabs on her page. Gather square bread-bag tabs; heat tab with heat gun. Tab will fold into itself forming a cylinder bead. Slip ribbon through curled tab. Adhere ribbon with curled tabs to page along border. Slip short piece of ribbon through curled tag and adhere to photo mat. If applicable, display expiration dates on curled tabs to document date of photos.

Mendy Douglass, Frankfort, Kentucky

Supplies Patterned papers and date stickers (Provo Craft); letter script stickers (NRN Designs); baby stickers (Creative Imaginations); metal-rimmed circle tags (American Tag); blue cardstock
Found Objects Bread-bag tabs; ribbon; rickrack; brads

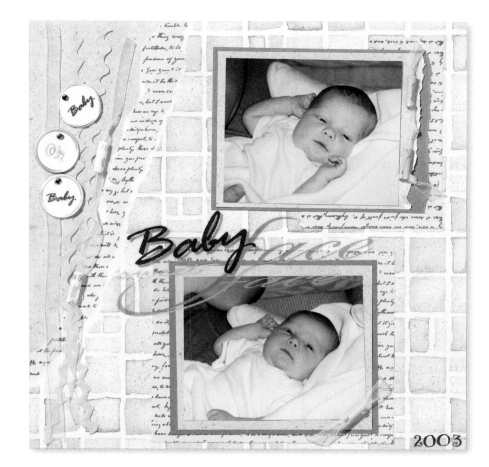

The Pink Tornado

USE A BOTTLE CAP AS AN EMBELLISHMENT

The pink Diet Squirt bottle cap seemed fitting for a page about Nikki's daughter, her little squirt who likes to wear pink. Select pink paper with swirls to complement theme. Adhere bottle cap to white mat. To create matching brad, emboss brad with pink embossing powder then attach to page.

Nikki Pitcher, Olympia, Washington

Supplies Pink patterned paper (American Crafts); letter stickers (Colorbök, Treehouse Designs, Wordsworth); embossing powder
Found Objects Bottle cap; brad

Snow Cute

MAKE SNOWFLAKES WITH COFFEE FILTERS AND CUPCAKE HOLDERS

Ginger created inexpensive snowflakes using paper items from her kitchen cupboard. To make snowflakes, fold round filter or cupcake holder in half, fold again from center point, fold one more time to create a triangle shape. Cut out small shapes on fold lines, open up to reveal unique snowflake. Adhere to page. Tie snowflake charms onto journaling block using embroidery floss. Consider using a foil cupcake holder for a metallic look on a holiday page.

Ginger McSwain, Cary, North Carolina

Supplies Snowflake charms (source unknown); dark and light blue cardstocks

Found Object Paper coffee filter; paper baking cupcake holders; embroidery floss

Snow Cute

Rachel & Samuel and their new frosty pal... He looks more solidly built than he apparently was. He made it for about an hour and then toppled over in our backyard.   1/09/04

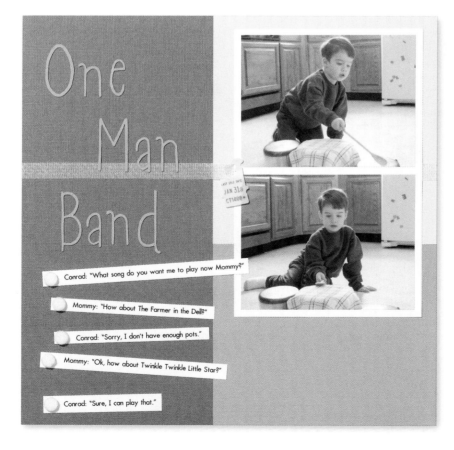

Conrad: "What song do you want me to play now Mommy?"

Mommy: "How about The Farmer in the Dell?"

Conrad: "Sorry, I don't have enough pots."

Mommy: "Ok, how about Twinkle Twinkle Little Star?"

Conrad: "Sure, I can play that."

One Man Band

DISCOVER PAGE ACCENTS IN JUNK DRAWER

Becky found an array of interesting page accents in her junk drawer for her layout showcasing a conversation with her son. Adhere gauze strip to page. Attach bread-bag tab to strip of gauze. Print journaling on white paper and cut into thin strips. Attach felt pads to strips to denote bullet points.

Becky Kent, Hilliard, Ohio

Supplies Blue, yellow, tan and white cardstocks

Found Objects Bread-bag tabs; gauze strip; felt pads for cabinets

Cherish

TRANSFORM DRAWER LINER
INTO TEXTURED BACKGROUND

Wanda created a masculine layout convey-
ing the ruggedness of the ancient fort in
the photo. Stamp kitchen drawer liner with
ink to add color and dimension. Mount on
background paper. Attach ribbon on top
of paper to create border. Decorate ribbon
with paper sunflowers. Adhere metal
plaque to page.

Wanda Santiago-Cintron, Deerfield, Wisconsin

Supplies Scrabble stickers and definition stickers (Making Memories);
blue cardstock
Found Objects Drawer liner; ribbon; paper sunflowers; metal plaque

Silly

ADD INTRIGUING TEXTURE
WITH PAPER TOWELS

Using paper towels and a marker, Wendy
discovered an inexpensive way to create
dimension and intrigue. Adhere strip of
drywall mesh to background paper. Tear
paper towel to create mats for photos.
Use brush tip marker to ink the edges;
adhere to page. Add photos. Write title
with marker then chalk over title. Attach
rocks to circle tag; thread string through
tag; adhere tag to mat made from drywall mesh.

Wendy Malichio, Bethel, Connecticut

Supplies Blue cardstock; blue brush tip marker; metal-rimmed circle tag
(Avery); chalk
Found Objects Paper towels; drywall mesh from hardware store;
metal clips; polished rocks; string

Repose
n. 1 A pause or moment of rest signaled by a familiar gesture of comfort. 2 You, a few days before turning ONE.
November 2003

APTER 2

Bed & Bath

The bedroom and bathroom are our comfort zones, tender havens of rest and relief for our busy lives. A typical person devotes approximately 40 percent of his or her daily time sleeping and taking care of personal hygiene. Whether it's enjoying a fitful slumber or a quick catnap, putting away laundry, reading in a luxurious bubble bath, grooming, staring at ourselves in the mirror or participating in germ warfare, time in the bedroom and bathroom can be well-spent—where scrapbooking is concerned—when you know what to look for.

While hanging out in your boudoir, sift through jewelry boxes and rummage through bureau drawers for broken jewelry, clothing labels, errant buttons, safety pins, shoelaces, small toys and other odds and ends that find their way to the bedroom when they have nowhere else to go. In the washroom, a quick raid can yield bandages, broken barrettes and bobby pins, compact mirrors, cotton swabs, dental floss, makeup applicators and product packaging with seemingly endless possibilities. And don't forget about old toothbrushes, powdered eyeshadow and shaving cream; they can be put to good use in your scrapbooks too.

Sleep and hygiene are certainly important, and cleaning can be downright drudgery. But with this chapter, make your bed and bath time most enjoyable by giving found items new zest on scrapbook pages that showcase your style and individuality!

It's not how many times we breathe that matters, It's how many times something takes our breath away.

Hannah

TURN A LOST BUTTON INTO A PAGE ACCENT

Diane found a button in the master bedroom and knew it would be an intriguing accent for a page featuring her grand-daughter. Adhere 12 x 6" piece of patterned paper to background paper. Center button below photo and attach with double-sided tape. Attach vellum journaling block to page with eyelets; tie with ribbon.

Diane Sanchez, Melbourne, Florida
Photo: Photography by Chez, Melbourne, Florida

Supplies Patterned pink paper (Hot Off The Press); patterned floral paper (K & Company); vellum; eyelets
Found Objects Spare button; ribbon

Found Treasures From the Bedroom & Bathroom

Bandages
Bobby pins
Broken barrettes and hair combs
Broken mirror shards
Broken watch components
Children's art
Clothing remnants and labels
Coloring and outgrown storybooks
Cotton balls and swabs
Dental floss

Dominoes
Extra clothing buttons
Makeup and applicators
Nail polish and decals
Old compacts
Old jewelry
Old jewelry-box hinges
Playing cards
Potpourri
Product packaging

Puzzle pieces
Rhinestones and crystals
Safety pins
Shoelaces
Small toys
Terry cloth remnants
Toy money and board-game pieces
Vintage handkerchiefs and gloves

Texturizing Cardstock

Drag a comb in patterns through wet paint on cardstock to create textured cardstocks. Use for background, borders, mats, frames or tags.

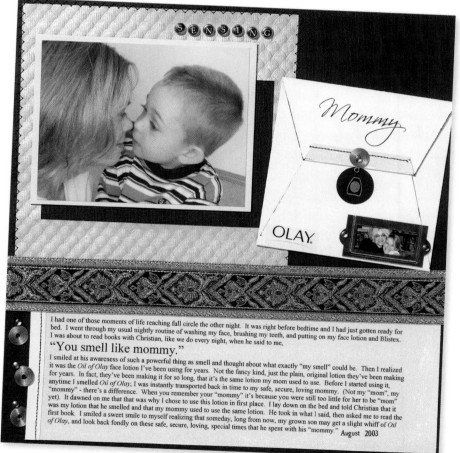

Sensing Mommy

TELL A STORY WITH A PACKAGE LABEL

When her young son commented on her familiar fragrance, Patricia knew he was referring to her Oil of Olay lotion. On her page, she used the Oil of Olay label to help tell the story. Select pink patterned paper and black cardstock to match the Oil of Olay packaging. Machine stitch silver paper, ribbon and journaling block onto black background paper. Print "Mommy" on pink cardstock then fold to create an envelope. Adhere product name and logo to envelope. Slip photo into label holder. Attach label holder to envelope with brads.

Patricia Anderson, Selah, Washington

Supplies Silver patterned paper (Emagination Crafts); pink patterned paper (Chatterbox); brads (Creative Imaginations); charms (7 Gypsies); envelope template (Deluxe Designs); circle punch; black cardstock
Found Objects Lotion bottle packaging; ribbon; label holder; brads; date stamp

Gertrude Dumphy

ADD AN ELEGANT TOUCH WITH A LACE GLOVE

A delicate lace glove was a fitting adornment for a page featuring a vintage photo Jane's grandpa shot, developed and colorized. Layer patterned paper on green background paper. Attach glove to page. Attach jewelry, purple sequin circle and filigree to glove. Accent photo corners with filigree. Use brads to attach label holder displaying date.

Jane Swanson, Janesville, Wisconsin

Supplies Floral patterned paper (Club Scrap); transparency; filigree (www.maudeandmillie.com); green cardstock
Found Objects Lace glove; jewelry; purple sequin circle; label holder

James and Gertrude

ADORN PAGE WITH LADY'S HANDKERCHIEF

Jane complemented a heritage photo of her grandparents by adding a lady's handkerchief along with other found objects. Fold lady's handkerchief and attach to patterned paper. Accent handkerchief with clock-face button, gold chain and filigree. Accent date with picture-hanging hardware.

Jane Swanson, Janesville, Wisconsin

Supplies Floral patterned paper (Club Scrap); filigree (www.maudeandmillie.com); green cardstock; transparency
Found Objects Handkerchief; clock-face button; chain; picture-hanging hardware

Faux Chalk

In a pinch, use powdered eyeshadow for chalk. Brush or spray lightly with rubbing alcohol to intensify colors.

Meetmop!

DISCOVER COLORANTS IN BATHROOM VANITY

Searching her bathroom vanity, Michelle found numerous colorants and creative solutions for a page about her daughter's fascination with makeup, or as she calls it, "meetmop." Use eye shadow to shade the edges of title, journaling blocks and tags. Stitch photo mats with dental floss, then dust edges with sparkling body powder and seal with nail polish. Shade strips of pink paper with blush and place over strips of white gauze. Use bobby pins to hold potpourri in place on title and journaling blocks; tie small tags to potpourri with dental floss. Accent top of page below with beaded headband.

Michelle Pesce, Arvada, Colorado

Supplies Pink patterned paper (Karen Foster Design); black and pink cardstocks
Found Objects First aid gauze; eye shadow; blush; dental floss; nail polish; sparkling baby powder; bobby pins; potpourri; beaded headband

Frugal Bonus Idea #6

Splatter Painting

Apply paint to a toothbrush and run your thumb across the brush for a paint-splattered effect on paper.

First Jean Skirt

PRINT TITLE ON DENIM

Using denim for her title was fitting for a page featuring Candi's daughter in her first jean skirt. Cut out piece of denim. Flatten and adhere denim to a piece of 8½ x 11" cardstock; tape down edges and run through printer. Remove denim from cardstock and adhere to pink cardstock. Layer worn hem over edge of title and accent photo mat with snaps to continue the clothing theme. Finish by attaching decorative ribbon through the center of the page.

Candi Gershon, Fishers, Indiana

Supplies Heart sticker (EK Success); metal tag and letter stamps (Foofala); light and dark pink cardstocks; brads
Found Objects Denim; ribbon; embroidery floss; snaps

Marinaberry Cupcake

TRANSFORM PRODUCT PACKAGING INTO A PHOTO FRAME

The colorful Strawberry Shortcake bubble bath packaging was the perfect frame for a fun page about Kathy's daughter Marina, known for her strawberry blonde curls. Cut out frame from bubble bath packaging. Trim pieces of foam into thin strips and adhere to back of frame. Silhouette photo of subject and layer with hat sticker and handcut clothing decorated with colored pencils. Adhere frame on top of decorated package backing.

Kathy Potter, New Market, Maryland

Supplies Pink patterned paper (EK Success); stickers (Strawberry Shortcake); pink mulberry paper; purple cardstock; vellum; colored pencils; eyelets
Found Objects Product packaging; foam wrapping; cookies and garden tool toys; ribbon

Shaving-Cream Painting

Put a thin layer of foam shaving cream on a plate and add drops of acrylic paint on top. Use a toothpick to swirl the paint drops lightly to create a marbleized effect in foam. Working in sections, lightly press cardstock facedown into mixture. Wipe off excess foam and paint with a paper towel in one stroke. Repeat as needed to cover cardstock and allow to dry.

Frugal Bonus Idea #7

Mom's Image

FIND NEW USES FOR ITEMS FROM THE BATHROOM

Linda created a vibrant and contemporary page using an array of items from her bathroom vanity. Color a 1¼" wide strip of paper with various shades of lipstick; layer with word stickers and an eye shadow applicator. Using various shades of eye shadow, color another strip. Add word sticker, eye shadow applicator and broken necklace to second strip; secure necklace with safety pins and add tassels to each end. For "hanging" journaling element, apply a bleach pen to jewelry card. Decorate card with word stickers, hot roller clip, charm and elastic hair band. Hang jewelry card on button with yarn. Create photo mat by layering pieces of toilet paper over blue cardstock; clip bobby pin to mat. Turn makeup applicator matchbook into a fold-out page element by adding letter stickers and a small mirror to the inside.

Linda Franklin, Ankeny, Iowa

Supplies Patterned paper (7 Gypsies); word stickers (Bo-Bunny Press, C-Thru Ruler); letter stickers (Paper Fever); black, blue and white cardstocks
Found Objects Lipstick; eye shadow, eye shadow applicators; makeup applicator matchbook; button; yarn; jewelry card; hot roller clip; charm; elastic hair band; mirror; safety pins; necklace; toilet paper; bobby pin

Meals are becoming more and more entertaining these days as our little drama king hones his acting skills. He seems to have inherited a love of the stage from his uncle Bill.

Depending on the day and his mood, he may or may not be interested in any of the food he is offered, and the looks of torture on his face as he sits trapped in the highchair make his feelings abundantly clear! With a little practice, we could have an Oscar winner on our hands!

SUMMER 2003

Dinner Theater

A PRODUCTION IN MANY ACTS
BY CONNOR CYRUS

Dinner Theater

SEARCH A JEWELRY BOX FOR PAGE ACCENTS

For a page about her son—"the drama king"—Susan found the ideal page accent in her jewelry box: theatrical mask pins. The gold color of the pins coordinates well with her son's yellow shirt. Remove backing from pins and adhere over thin strip of dark blue paper.

Susan Cyrus, Broken Arrow, Oklahoma

Supplies Patterned paper (Chatterbox); letter stamps (All Night Media; Hero Arts); light blue and dark blue cardstocks; black stamping ink; vellum
Found Objects Theatrical mask pins

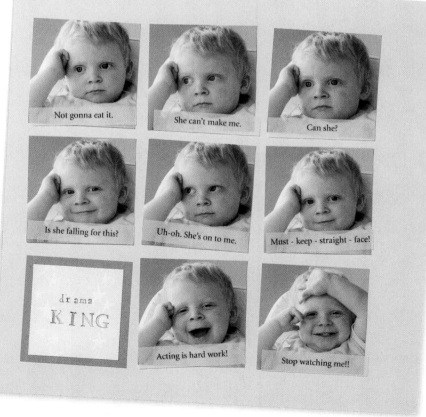

Not gonna eat it.

She can't make me.

Can she?

Is she falling for this?

Uh-oh. She's on to me.

Must - keep - straight - face!

drama KING

Acting is hard work!

Stop watching me!!

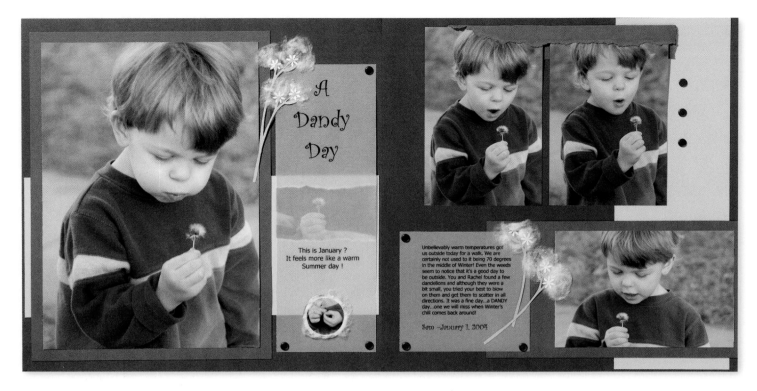

A Dandy Day

CREATE DANDELIONS WITH COTTON BALLS

With a little ingenuity, Ginger discovered that cotton balls could easily resemble dandelions for a page featuring her son picking the real thing. Tone down the cotton balls' brightness by applying tan chalk. Spread cotton apart and add premade paper flowers with leaves removed. Adhere chalked cotton ball on top of metal-rimmed tag to carry the theme through.

Ginger McSwain, Cary, North Carolina

Supplies Premade flowers (EK Success); vellum; blue, tan and olive cardstocks; metal-rimmed tag; snaps
Found Objects Cotton balls

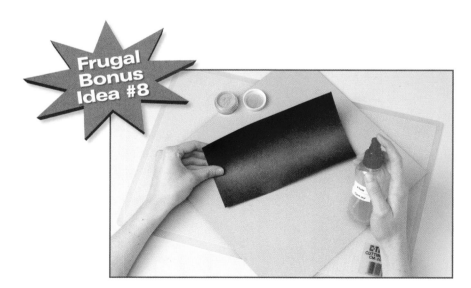

Frugal Bonus Idea #8

Making Paper Shimmer

Mix pigment powder in a bottle with hairspray and spritz over cardstock to give it a unique metallic shine.

Little Man

USE A BROOCH AND EARRINGS TO MATCH A CHILD'S OUTFIT

Ruthann used nautical jewelry to complement a photo of her son in a sailor suit. Bend back post on sailboat earrings and mount on small squares of yellow and blue cardstock. Pin matching brooch through larger cardstock squares. Adhere elements vertically for a border.

Ruthann Grabowski, Yorktown, Virginia

Supplies Phrase sticker (EK Success); blue and yellow cardstocks
Found Objects Nautical brooch and earrings

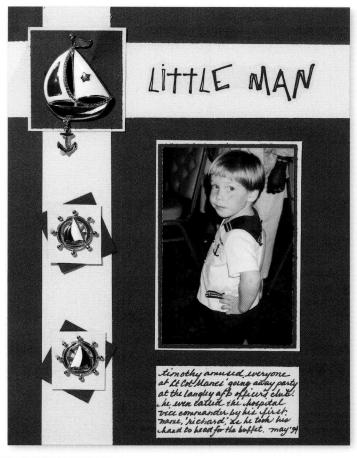

Let It Snow

ACCENT A PHOTO MAT WITH OLD EARRINGS

What does one do with earrings from several decades ago? Ruthann used them to decorate her photo mat on a winter-themed page. Attach a single dangling earring to a snowflake earring and adhere to the top left corner of photo mat. Mount other snowflake earring on the opposite bottom corner.

Ruthann Grabowski, Yorktown, Virginia

Supplies Tan snowflake patterned paper (Daisy D's); blue snowflake patterned paper (source unknown); blue word patterned paper (Carolee's Creations); phrase sticker (EK Success); plum cardstock
Found Objects Dangling earring; snowflake earrings

My Not-So-Girly Girl

USE A NECKLACE AS A BORDER

When Lisa came across an old bead necklace in her jewelry box that her daughter used to play with, she knew it would be great for a page about her daughter's changing looks and interests. Trim edges of lavender paper, adhere necklace around outer edges. Mat lavender with sage green and dark purple cardstocks. String extra beads onto a hoop earring; place earring around one word of title for emphasis. Add heart earring near hoop.

Lisa Dixon, East Brunswick, New Jersey

Supplies Dark purple, lavender, green and white cardstocks; vellum; black pen
Found Objects Bead necklace; heart earring; hoop earring

Art

CREATE PAPER WITH CHILD'S SCRIBBLES

Rosemary found a new use for the drawing her daughter created on her Magnadoodle toy: inexpensive yet imaginative patterned paper! Take a digital photo of the drawing. Convert it to black and white on the computer and print it on white cardstock. Layer purple vellum over part of the drawing for added interest.

Rosemary Waits, Mustang, Oklahoma

Supplies Patterned paper (7 Gypsies); purple vellum; lavender and white cardstocks
Found Objects Children's artwork

Precious Jewels

USE A SCARF AS A PAGE BACKGROUND

Paula's dressmaking experience proved to be useful when trying to fit a large scarf onto a smaller area. To create the puckered background, staple a scarf to the corners and sides of cardstock. Gently fold and staple the remaining loose fabric in place. Cut a frame from another piece of 12 x 12" cardstock, place over page and machine stitch to reinforce edges. Hand stitch pearl necklace to page. Hang a small chain necklace around brads and secure heart pendant in place with adhesive.

Paula Frances Jones, Caledon, Ontario, Canada

Supplies Heart-shaped jewel (ScrapSmart); green cardstock; thread; gold paper; transparency; brads
Found Objects Green scarf; pearl necklace; chain

The World's Most Beautiful Mother

USE UPHOLSTERY REMNANT FOR A BACKGROUND

Rozanne discovered an appropriate background for a heritage page in her collection of upholstery remnants. In addition, she accented this photo of her mother with her mother's hair comb from high school and a vintage button from her mother's sewing kit. Cover cardstock with upholstery remnant. Make photo stand out by mounting it on a piece of cardstock wrapped in linen. Attach fringe and accent with vintage button. Randomly loop upholstery cord on page then stitch in place; add hair comb. String buttons together and attach to cord. Write title on transparency and secure to linen scrap using eyelets.

Rozanne Paxman, West Jordan, Utah

Supplies Tag and clip (Making Memories); glaze; brown cardstock; transparency; black pen; eyelets
Found Objects Upholstery remnant; upholstery cord and fringe; hair comb; vintage button; linen; acrylic paint

Discovery of Nature

COLOR TOILET PAPER WITH SUNLESS TANNING LOTION

Shandy colored toilet paper with sunless tanning lotion to achieve a rich brown leatherlike look. When applying the lotion to paper, wear gloves to prevent staining hands. Let paper dry completely after applying. To expedite the drying process, use a hair dryer. Mount colored toilet paper to background and green photo mat; layer with journaling tag and photograph. Stamp title letters using tanning lotion as an inking medium. To add dimension to the journaling tag, ink the edges with tanning lotion as well.

Shandy Vogt, Nampa, Idaho

Supplies Letter stamps (Stampin' Up!); pendant charm (Li'l Davis Designs); letter sticker (EK Success); tan and green cardstocks; black pen; mesh; eyelets; vellum; fibers

Found Objects Toilet paper; sunless tanning lotion; thread

Maysie Style

ADD STYLE WITH CLOTHING LABELS

With a handful of labels from her daughter's clothing, Mellette quickly and inexpensively conveyed her daughter's fashion sense on this page. Cut labels from clothing. Frame one label with yellow cardstock. Attach all labels and metal shoe tag to a piece of 4½ x 6" yellow cardstock. Place premade frame over yellow cardstock to highlight labels.

Mellette Berezoski, Crosby, Texas

Supplies Yellow patterned papers (KI Memories, Magenta); premade frame and flower (My Mind's Eye); letter stickers (Creative Imaginations, EK Success); flower charm (www.twopeasina bucket.com); date stamp

Found Objects Clothing labels; metal shoe tag; yarn

What We LOVE About The Easter Bunny

We love how **cuddly** the bunny is and we love how **cute** the bunny is too. We love that the bunny is a sign of warm **Spring** weather on it's way and we love beautiful **baskets** of decorated **eggs**. We love the grass of **green** and we love **pink** and **yellow** too. There are so many reasons to LOVE the Easter Bunny, but we think the **best reason** of all to love the Easter Bunny is for the CANDY he brings us on Easter morning!

Rachel –anxiously awaiting Easter treats April 21, 2000

What We Love About the Easter Bunny

DECORATE PAGE WITH THEMED ERASERS

Inside her daughter's craft box, Ginger discovered Easter-themed erasers and colorful markers. She found a use for all of them on this Easter page. Punch squares from light green paper; adhere erasers to squares. Print journaling on light green cardstock. Highlight key words in journaling block using different colored markers.

Ginger McSwain, Cary, North Carolina

Supplies Patterned paper (It Takes Two); cream and light green cardstocks; square punch
Found Objects Erasers; markers

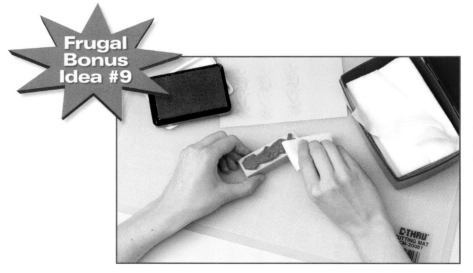

Frugal Bonus Idea #9

Cleaning Rubber Stamps

Press pre-moistened hand towelettes or baby wipes onto rubber stamps to clean them.

Read Me a Story

RETRIEVE A FAVORITE BOOK FROM TOY BOX

When Ruthann found a little children's book at the bottom of her son's toy box, she combined it with a 10-year-old photo of her reading the same book to her kids. The book is small enough that it does not weigh down the page and can still be read each time the layout is viewed. Attach small book to layout using strong adhesive. Mark child's favorite page with a square of yellow paper.

Ruthann Grabowski, Yorktown, Virginia

Supplies Title and storybook images (EK Success); book sticker (Colorbök); light green, rust and yellow cardstocks; black and green pens
Found Object Children's book

New Hat

ADD WHIMSY WITH CHILDREN'S BOOK ILLUSTRATIONS

Gemiel's son loves reading about the hats in the children's book *Go Dog Go* by P.D. Eastman. Illustrations from the book were the perfect page accent when her son got a new hat of his own. To match the hat, cut a piece of green felt and fringe the edges with scissors, then use as a photo mat. Attach green yarn to hat's price tag and place tag in a small vellum pocket.

Gemiel Matthews, Yorktown, Virginia

Supplies Metal letter tags (Provo Craft); metal-rimmed tag (Making Memories); vellum pocket (Colorbök); burgundy and blue cardstocks; brads
Found Objects Children's book illustrations; price tag; green felt

Faux Rubber Stamps

To create your own rubber stamps, heat a foam bath toy with a light bulb or a heat-embossing gun and press the warmed foam onto something with texture: an ornate drawer pull, a pile of paper clips or rubber bands, etc. The stamp will provide an embossed-like image and the foam will retain its shape until heated again.

Lego

BUILD A BORDER WITH LEGOS

Ruthann used her son's Lego blocks to create a colorful and dimensional border for a page about a visit to the Lego Imagination Center in Downtown Disney. To create border, gather various colors of Lego blocks. Line them up around edges of page and use strong adhesive to adhere blocks to cardstock. Adhere two more blocks in the center of the page.

Ruthann Grabowski, Yorktown, Virginia

Supplies Green, red, blue, yellow and white cardstocks; black pen; foam tape

Found Objects Lego blocks

Magical Things

LET CHILDREN GATHER FOUND OBJECTS

To create this page, Lana asked her son to find five things in his bedroom that represent him. He came back with a handful of items that made interesting and telling page accents. She added a poem about magical things one might find in a boys' pocket. On right page, color five small tags with brown chalk. Thread string through holes and attach to page with brads. Mount tags on background and adhere found items to each tag. Write descriptions of items on the tags.

Lana Rickabaugh, Maryville, Missouri

Supplies Stamped letters (Close To My Heart); brown stamping ink; chalk; heart punch; poem (www.twopeasinabucket.com); slide mount; dark green and tan cardstocks; mesh; black pen; brads
Found Objects Quarter; Beanie Baby tag; football team sticker; plastic lizard; arrowhead; tags; string

Cousins at Play

ACCENT WITH PUZZLE PIECES AND A PLAYING CARD

Puzzle pieces and a playing card were the perfect way for Ruthann to enhance a layout featuring children playing games. Accent corners of photos and title with puzzle pieces. Slip playing card between one photo and its mat to reinforce the game theme.

Ruthann Grabowski, Yorktown, Virginia

Supplies Puzzle patterned paper (Club Scrap); preprinted title (My Mind's Eye); black pen; plum and tan cardstocks
Found Objects Puzzle pieces; playing card

Perfection

EMBELLISH PLAYING CARDS

Joanne dressed up her page by adding tiny playing cards that she embellished. Dab ink pad over cards; stamp with heart and postage stamps. Heat emboss stamped images. Apply embossing ink pen around edges of cards, sprinkle with embossing powder and heat emboss as well. Accent cards with small gems. To match the red background of the cards, Joanne applied chalk to white cardstock for her background.

Joanne Moseley, Aurora, Ontario, Canada

Supplies Red textured paper (Creative Imaginations); heart stamp (Close To My Heart); faux postage stamp (Inkadinkado); embossing ink pen (Tsukineko); white cardstock; chalk; terra cotta stamping ink; embossing ink; gold embossing powder
Found Objects Playing cards; ribbon; gems

Louise

MAKE COLOR COPIES OF TREASURED MEMENTOS

To make a tribute page for her mom, Christine gathered items from her mom's sewing kit and jewelry box. To prevent bulk and to preserve the original items, Christine scanned the items and returned them to her keepsake chest. She also attached parts of her father's old watch to the page. Make color copies of mementos. Trim images and adhere to tag and small paper squares. Tie fibers through tag and attach matching button; tear bottom edge. Adhere watch parts to page.

Christine Chapman, Torrance, California
Photo: David W. Chapman, Atkinson, New Hampshire

Supplies Pink patterned paper, snaps, precut oval (Chatterbox); vellum; light purple cardstock; tag; embroidery floss
Found Objects Pin; lace; rickrack; key; buttons; postage stamp; watch parts

APTER 3

Home Office

Today's budget-friendly technology and contemporary product has brought the office home for just about everyone, whether you have a full-time day job or not. But you may be surprised to know that only about 1.5 hours per day of work actually goes on in the home office. The rest of the time is spent socializing, pursuing personal interests, reading junk mail, eating, playing computer games, engaging in nonbusiness communication, shuffling papers and doing lots of other non-work tasks. But, by gosh, we have the best-stocked home offices around in case we decide to forget about work and do some scrapbooking.

The next time you're staring at the computer or waiting for that eight-page fax to come through, make idle hands productive. Scan all drawers, bins, shelves and file cabinets for those needful things that you have in abundance: brads, coin holders, date stamps, file folders, labels, maps, old greeting cards, paper clips, rubber bands, stamps and staples. Zero in on that old typewriter, paper shredder and CD-ROM for use in your scrapbooks too.

Just as there is an art to managing time, there is an art to growing a discerning eye for found items that can be put to work in a scrapbook. With a little labor and the contents of this chapter, you'll never look at your office contents the same again!

Puppy Dog Eyes

PRINT JOURNALING ON ADDRESS LABELS

Terrie printed her journaling on a strip of self-adhesive address labels to create a compelling yet simple layout about her dog's soulful eyes. Print journaling on labels; layer over patterned papers. Attach small preprinted tag to journaling with a brad. Add paper clip to focal-point photo and attach binder clip to secondary photo.

Terrie McDaniel, League City, Texas

Supplies Patterned papers (KI Memories); letter stickers (Creative Imaginations, Li'l Davis Designs, Wordsworth); preprinted tag (Sticker Studio); green cardstock; brad
Found Objects Address labels; binder clip; paper clip

Found Treasures From the Home Office

Address labels
Brads
Business cards
Calendars
Canceled postage stamps
Coin holders
Corkboard
Date stamps
Dictionary pages
Eyeglass screws
File-folder and index tabs
File-folder clasps

File folders
Film-canister lids
Index cards
Junk mail
Label-maker labels
Labels
Maps
Negative strips
Old CD-ROMs
Old greeting cards
Paper and binder clips
Postcards

Reinforcements
Rubber bands
Rulers
Small change or foreign coins
Small envelopes
Staples
Sticky notes
Tags
Ticket stubs

Enjoy the Journey

Tracy had some negatives that she wouldn't need for reprints, so used them as page accents. Staple one negative strip behind premade quote and adhere to page. Slip second negative strip behind photo and accent with word stickers.

Tracy Johnson, Memory Makers Advertising Staff Photos: Hank Smith Photography, Westminster, Colorado

Supplies Green patterned paper, letter, tag and word stickers (Pebbles); letter stamps (Hero Arts); quote (Hot Off The Press); tan and light green cardstocks; twill tape; black stamping ink

Found Objects Negative strips; staples

Crop Quest

ENHANCE A PAGE WITH A BUSINESS CARD

Laura added her husband's business logo and name to a layout highlighting his career as an agronomist. For journaling, she included the company's mission statement. Tear logo and name from business card; chalk edges. Adhere torn pieces to top and bottom of photo. Copy mission statement from back of business card and print on brown cardstock.

Laura Wolff, Pawnee Rock, Kansas

Supplies Patterned paper (Leaving Prints); brown, green, purple and yellow cardstocks; square punch; chalk; brads; foam tape

Found Objects Business card

Chugga-Chugga-Choo-Choo

DISCOVER COLORFUL ITEMS IN OFFICE DESK DRAWERS

Searching their office desk drawers, Jodi and MaryJo discovered an array of office items in primary colors to use on this page featuring Colorado's Tiny Town Railway. The primary colors convey a sense of childlike wonder that kids feel when they ride a train. Use label maker to create a red 12" top border and a blue 12" bottom border. Repeat page title across border. Adhere to page. Mount all photos on foam core board and adhere to page. Slide date label into red index tab then attach to photo mat. Loop red, yellow and blue rubber bands around smaller photos. Accent page with train-themed postage stamps, tickets from train ride, paper clips and tacks.

Jodi Amidei, Memory Makers Books
Photos: MaryJo Regier, Memory Makers Books

Supplies Patterned paper (Deluxe Designs, Pebbles); vellum; foam core board
Found Objects Label maker; index tab; postage stamps; tickets from train ride; rubber bands; tacks; paper clips

Inside Joke

ATTACH FILE FOLDER TABS TO HIDDEN JOURNALING

Angela used found objects from her office to create a cheerful layout featuring inside jokes between her and a longtime friend. Paint four mini envelopes with yellow, green, blue and red paint and adhere to page. Create a small journaling block for each joke. Label file folder tabs with joke topics and attach to the top of each journaling block. Accent envelopes with rubber band and paper clips.

Angela Marvel, Puyallup, Washington

Supplies Letter stamps (source unknown); metal corner accents (Making Memories); red, white and yellow cardstocks; paint
Found Objects File folder tabs and labels; mini envelopes; paper clips; rubber band

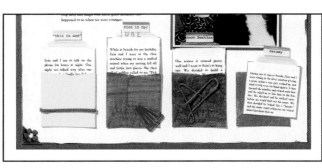

The Colors of Disney

CREATE A COLORFUL BORDER WITH
FILE DIVIDERS AND PAPER CLIPS

Kathy brought the magic of Disney to her page using transparent file dividers and paper clips. Print title vertically on white cardstock. Adhere title strip to left page. Cut blue, green, purple, orange and yellow transparency file dividers into 2 x 2" squares. Punch holes through top and bottom of squares and add hole reinforcements. Color reinforcements to match transparencies. Hook dividers together with colored paper clips. Place over title strip and clip to page. Create a different colored mat for each photo. Attach matching tabs from file folders with photo captions inside. Cut rectangles from transparent file dividers and adhere over various words below photos.

Kathy Fesmire, Athens, Tennessee

Supplies Patterned paper (Deluxe Designs); black, blue, green, purple, orange, yellow and white cardstocks; colored pens

Found Objects Transparent file folders with tabs; hole reinforcements; paper clips

The Greatest Use of a Life

JOURNAL ON NOTEBOOK PAPER

Vanessa personalized a page of her husband and son by writing a note to them on notebook paper. Using a black pen, write message in ruled spiral notebook. Tear paper out of notebook and tear into two pieces. Ink edges of both pieces and adhere to page. Use paper clips to accent one piece of notebook paper and to attach vellum quote to layout. To create binding on photo mat, fold over edges of mat, staple and thread string through holes.

Vanessa Spady, Virginia Beach, Virginia

Supplies Patterned papers (Chatterbox, Rusty Pickle); vellum quote (DieCuts with a View); stickers (Sticker Studio); cocoa stamping ink; dark blue cardstock; buttons
Found Objects Notebook paper; string; staples; paper clips

Frugal Bonus Idea #11

Shredding Photos & Paper

Use a paper shredder to crop photos into slices and reassemble as new photo art or shred colored cardstock into strips for paper weaving or for quilling.

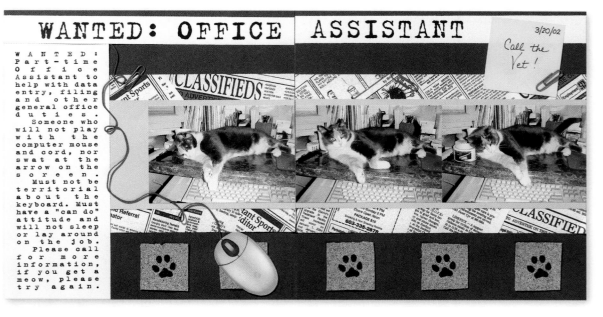

Wanted: Office Assistant

CREATE A CORKBOARD BORDER

When Rebecca realized her cat was not much help at the office, she wrote an engaging classified ad for a new assistant. To reinforce the office theme, she added a few found objects from the office including corkboard, electrical wire, paper clips, a section of the newspaper and a self-stick note. Copy classified ad section, cut into strips and adhere to page. Cut 2" cork squares from old corkboard. Use paw-print stencil and black pen to color paw prints onto cork. Photograph computer mouse, print on photo paper and silhouette crop. Randomly curl red wire and attach to page as the mouse's cable. Accent page with self-stick note and red paper clips.

Rebecca Chabot, Sanford, Maine

Supplies Dark green, tan and gray flecked cardstocks
Found Objects Newspaper; red electrical wire; computer mouse; corkboard; self-stick note; paper clips

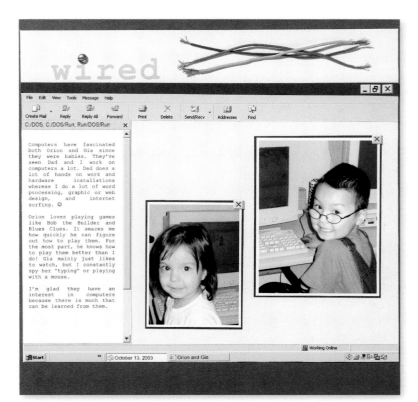

Wired

ADD WIRE FOR A HIGH-TECH LOOK

For a page about her computer-savvy children, Monica created a computer-style layout and used wires for embellishment. To create computer screen, use graphics software to modify a screen shot of an e-mail program. Personalize by adding the correct date and children's names. Print the screen shot or screen capture and adhere to cardstock. Use strong adhesive to attach frayed electrical wires to top of page.

Monica Kornfeld, Fairbanks, Alaska

Supplies Screw eyelet (Making Memories); dark blue, gray and white cardstocks; image-editing software
Found Object Electrical wires

Faux Sticker Letters & Typewriter Fonts

Type your journaling blocks with an old typewriter for a popular font look or photograph the keys, punch them out and use for title letters.

Working Girl

USE A BUSINESS CARD AS A DESIGN ELEMENT

With a business card and a photo from the office, Terrie conveyed her thoughts about her management position on this layout. Staple transparency to black paper and adhere over patterned and textured background. Use paper clip to attach business card to transparency. Print journaling on blank label paper and adhere to page.

Terrie McDaniel, League City, Texas

Supplies White textured paper (source unknown); red patterned paper, phrase stickers and letter stickers (Wordsworth); bubble letters (Li'l Davis Designs); keyboard letters and patterned transparency (Creative Imaginations); black and red cardstocks

Found Objects Business card; label sheets; paper clip; ribbon; staples

Kids' Christmas

PAINT CORRUGATED CARDBOARD

Janel conveyed the excitement of making Christmas goodies by "frosting" pieces of corrugated cardboard. To create frosted effect, brush white paint on corrugated cardboard. Cut cardboard into various sized squares and rectangles and use to mat photos, title letters and to decorate tag. For capital K, cut letter shape from a piece of painted chip board. Using label maker, type in descriptive words and adhere across corners of photos.

Janel Brown, Longmont, Colorado

Supplies Metal letters (Making Memories); red patterned paper (source unknown); tag punch (EK Success); letter stencil (Duro); rub-on words (Scrap Ease); moose buttons (source unknown); transparency; light, medium and dark green cardstocks; white acrylic paint; brad
Found Objects Corrugated cardboard; chip board; label maker; ribbon; hemp cord

Bailey

TRANSFORM A FILM-CANISTER LID

Mendy stamped into a plastic film-canister lid to create a faux wax seal for this page. To create seal, place gray film canister lid on a nonstick craft sheet in a well-ventilated area. Heat lid with embossing gun for about ten seconds—the lid will start to melt and shrink. Immediately stamp image into the melted plastic, leaving stamp embedded in plastic for several minutes until it is cool to the touch. Color with metallic rub-ons and red stamping ink. Attach fibers to draw one's eye to the seal.

Mendy Douglass, Frankfort, Kentucky
Photo: Claudia Hackbart, Frankfort, Kentucky

Supplies Black patterned paper (Paper Adventures); red patterned paper (Colorbök); letter stickers (Wordsworth); definition (Foofala); black cardstock; metallic rub-ons; red stamping ink; fibers
Found Objects Film-canister lid

Beautiful in Bibs

JOURNAL ON AN ENVELOPE

Kimberly displayed her journaling in a unique way by printing it on an envelope and inking the edges to give it definition. Staple pastel patterned paper to background paper. Print journaling on 8½ x 11" paper. Position envelope over printed text using temporary adhesive and run page through printer again. Remove envelope from paper, ink edges, stamp date and adhere to page. Ink edges of small, computer-printed tags to coordinate with the envelope.

Kimberly DeLong, Fremont, Michigan

Supplies Pastel patterned papers (Rusty Pickle); black cardstock; black stamping ink; tags; brads
Found Objects Envelope; date stamp; staples

Shhh....Serenity

HIGHLIGHT A PHOTO WITH
METAL FILE FASTENERS

Monica used a metal file fastener to accentuate her black-and-white photo. Print photo with white border and attach two binder reinforcements on top edge. Insert a metal file fastener through the holes. Accent tag with various metal embellishments to coordinate with the photo mat.

Monica Kornfeld, Fairbanks, Alaska

Supplies Striped patterned paper and circle die cuts (KI Memories); metal tab embellishments (Foofala); metal-rimmed tags (Making Memories); clock embellishment (7 Gypsies); concho (Scrapworks); pink, tan and off-white cardstocks; brown and black stamping ink; black cord; brad
Found Objects Metal file fasteners; hole reinforcements; paint chip

Giovanna Anne

DECORATE A COMPACT DISC

Janetta turned a junk-mail CD into a page decoration and creative backdrop for photos of her niece. Brush green acrylic paints over entire back surface of CD. When dry, brush with pink paint. Circle crop and mat photos to fit on the CD and accent with epoxy stickers.

Janetta Abucejo Wieneke, Memory Makers Books
Photos: Jonathan Abucejo, Copley, Ohio

Supplies Letter stickers and printed transparency (Memories Complete); epoxy stickers (K & Company); circle and square punches (EK Success); circle cutter (Fiskars); acrylic paints (Delta, Making Memories); pink, black and green cardstocks; eyelets

Found Objects Junk CD-ROM

Frugal Bonus Idea #13

Using Junk CDs

Use a junk CD-ROM as a paint palette, turn it into altered art or use it as a circle template.

Cutie

STAPLE A PHOTO MAT

Andrea embellished a photo mat with staples, then added a border of safety pins to coordinate. Brush white paint on edges of photo and green and purple mats; staple the two mats together, angling stapler sideways. Paint edges of green and purple strips for border. Insert snaps through safety pins; hammer snaps in place to attach pins to page.

Andrea Graves, Sandy, Utah

Supplies Purple and green patterned papers (Chatterbox); metal letters (Making Memories); letter stamps (PSX Design); purple stamping ink; white acrylic paint; white cardstock; snaps
Found Objects Safety pins; staples

May You Always

DISCOVER A NEW USE FOR AN OFFICE STAPLER

Robyn created a page with an inspirational message, accenting her border with a few simple staples. Randomly staple ¼" black cardstock strip to background paper. Use brads to attach metal letters to three small cardstock squares. Use label maker to create the word "always" and adhere to piece of patterned paper.

Robyn Ricks, LaSalle, Ontario, Canada

Supplies Striped paper (KI Memories); metal letters and wire words (Making Memories); white, burgundy, blue and green cardstocks; square punches; brads
Found Objects Staples; label maker

My Home

Heather captured her strong feelings for her hometown with a map highlighted with a metal ring, a few photos and heartfelt journaling. Download map from Internet and print in sepia. Create metal ring by removing paper from a metal-rimmed tag. Apply ring to page to highlight hometown. Add small family photo and numerous scenic photos from the area.

Heather Melzer, Yorkville, Illinois

Supplies Tan patterned paper (Anna Griffin); vellum; metal-rimmed circle tag and wire heart charm (Making Memories); brown cardstock

Found Object Map

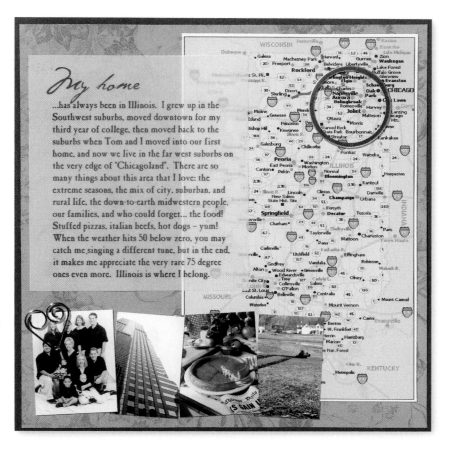

The Grandpa Files

Katherine used a file folder tab and self-stick notes to reveal all the reasons her daughter Mackenzie loves her grandfather. Cut file folder shape from striped background paper and attach file folder tab. Slide title strip into tab. Ink edges of envelope with brown stamping ink and adhere to file folder. Attach self-stick notes to 8½ x 11" paper with removable tape and run through printer to add journaling to the notes. Insert notes in envelope.

Katherine Teague, New Westminster, British Columbia, Canada

Supplies Patterned paper (SEI); alphabet stickers (Chatterbox); circle rub-on (Creative Imaginations); blue gray cardstock; brown stamping ink; brad

Found Objects File folder tab; self-stick notes; envelope; metal-rimmed tag

While You
Were Sleeping

SUPPORT AN INVESTIGATIVE THEME
WITH FILE FOLDERS AND PAPER CLIPS

Candi documented her son's morning
escapade of raiding the Halloween candy
stash with photos and descriptive, humorous
journaling. To create evidence bag, stamp
front of small brown bag then stuff with
candy wrappers. For "coffee" stain, dip bottom of plastic cup into walnut ink and press
onto page. Use label maker to identify each
"exhibit." Insert piece of patterned paper
into file folder. Adhere upper section of
folder to page. Accent page with safety pin
and paper clips.

Candi Gershon, Fishers, Indiana

Supplies Patterned paper (Chatterbox); letter stickers (Paper Fever); letter stamps
(PSX Design); number stickers (Karen Foster Design); square paper clips and
photo anchors (Making Memories); dark, light green and black cardstocks; black
stamping ink; walnut ink
Found Objects Candy wrappers; small brown paper bag; file folder; label maker;
date stamp; paper clips; safety pin

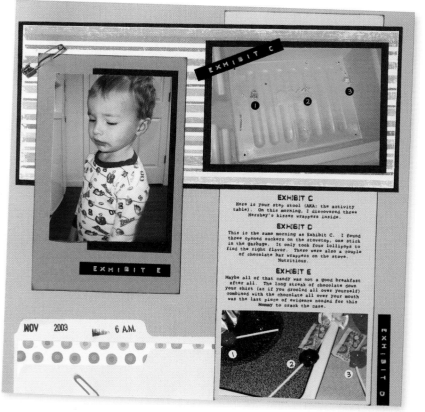

My Studio

FORM TITLE LETTERS WITH STAPLES

Holle used an array of office supplies to accentuate the theme of her page: her exciting career in scrapbooking. Spray walnut ink on crumpled calendar pages and notebook paper, trim as needed and layer on page. Use label maker to create descriptive journaling and adhere over calendar pages. Attach memorandum to top right corner with paper clips. To create title, use strips of clear tape to form the word "my" on an index card, then cover tape with metallic rub-ons. Use staples to form the word "studio" on six circles with inked edges. Journal on self-stick notes and adhere down left side of page. Apply brown chalk to index card, memorandum and self-stick notes.

Holle Wiktorek, Reunion, Colorado

Supplies Black and brown cardstocks; walnut ink; foam tape; chalk; metallic rub-ons; sepia stamping ink; circle punch; black and brown pens
Found Objects Calendar pages; memorandum; index card; self-stick notes; label maker; staples; clear tape; paper clips

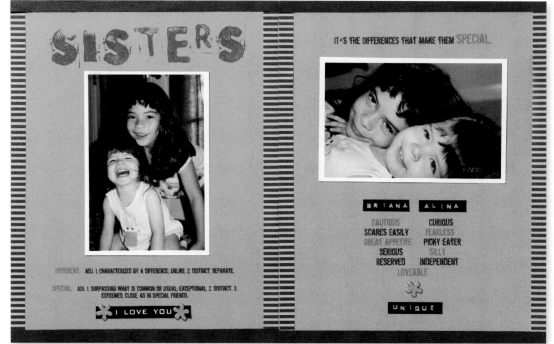

Sisters

USE LABEL MAKER TO ACCENTUATE WORDS

To empower her daughters, Anna created a page that highlights their unique qualities. The black label-maker backgrounds on tan cardstock allow their names to stand out above the descriptive words. Type out girls' names and the word "unique" with a label maker and adhere to layout.

Anna Estrada Davison, Cedar Park, Texas

Supplies Striped patterned paper (7 Gypsies); letter stamps (Ma Vinci's Reliquary); ribbon phrase and flower charms (Making Memories); brown stamping ink; brown and tan cardstocks
Found Object Label maker

APTER 4

Craft Room

In-home craft rooms are as capricious and distinctive as the treasures that are designed in them. And few rooms in a house can boast that their masters spend the most time there doing what they truly love: creating! Whether you sew, quilt, sculpt, paint or build models, you surround yourself with the tools, supplies and inspiration devoted to your creative pursuits. Honing your decorative craft can be as simple as spreading fabric swatches all around you on the floor in search of an exact color match or reworking a piece of clay in pursuit of the perfect texture for a given project. Regardless of your artistic medium, your craft room already stocks an abundance of things that will enhance your scrapbook page designs.

The next time you lose yourself in your personal playground, take a few moments to contemplate your artsy belongings again with the scrutiny of a scrapbook artist. You'll find boxes and baskets brimming with appliqués, beads, buttons, clay, fabric remnants, feathers, felt, fringe, paints, ribbon, rickrack and embroidery threads just waiting to find their way into your albums. Sewing notions such as hook-and-eye fasteners, measuring tapes, pins and needles—even old patterns and zippers— make great scrapbook page additions.

Your craft room provides you with a sacred environment in which you can relax, create and—yes—even dream a little. And with this chapter here and a stitch or two there, you'll sharpen your skills with simple, fast and stylish scrapbook solutions straight from your craft room.

Hey Handsome

EMBELLISH PAGE WITH STAINED GLASS

The gleaming pieces of stained glass from Valerie's craft room were a stunning embellishment for a page featuring portrait shots of her son, Addison. Gather pieces of stained glass in various shades of green. Use strong adhesive to adhere pieces of stained glass to page.

Valerie Barton, Flowood, Mississippi

Supplies Cream patterned paper (Creative Imaginations); metal frame (K & Company); photo corner and date stamp (Making Memories); letter stickers (Leisure Arts); brown stamping ink; cream cardstock; cream vellum;
Found Objects Pieces of stained glass

Found Treasures From the Sewing & Craft Room

Appliqués and patches
Beads
Buttons
Colored sand, sea glass and other craft supplies
Cotton batting
Crocheting, darning and knitting needles
Elastic
Embroidery threads
Fabric remnants
Feathers
Felt
Fringe

Gift wrap and gift bags
Hook-and-eyes fasteners
Lace
Measuring tape
Needle threader
Old patterns
Pins and needles
Plastic-coated wire hangers
Pompoms
Ribbon
Rickrack
Rivets

Seam bias tape
Sewing notions
Sewing supply packaging
Silk flowers
Snaps
Tassels
Tissue paper
Upholstery grommets
Velcro
Yarn
Zippers

In Memory Of

TELL A HEARTFELT STORY WITH SILK FLOWERS

For a page about the seasonal floral arrangements Janetta makes to honor her dad, she used leftover silk flowers from the floral arrangement in the photo and leftover ribbon from her wedding flower arrangement. To make left border, adhere ribbon to page. To accent small photo, make three folds on each side of ribbon to resemble a bow and place photo over center of ribbon. Use a small leaf die-cut and ribbon to create small leaves. Accent page with leaves and silk flowers.

Janetta Abucejo Wieneke, Memory Makers Books

Supplies Cloud-patterned vellum (DMD); letter stickers (Colorbök); small leaf die-cut (Sizzix); brown cardstock; watermark ink (Tsukineko); glitter embossing powder
Found Objects Silk flowers; ribbon

Learning How to Crochet

INTERWEAVE A LESSON WITH CROCHETING

MaryJo created an endearing page that recaptures her son's first crochet lesson. While her son went on to make a hacky-sack ball, MaryJo snatched up a few chain-stitched samples from their lesson for her layout. To create border, adhere 4" strip of tan patterned paper to green background paper. Attach three torn photos with chalked edges then punch two holes on top and bottom of border. Thread green crocheted chain through top holes, weave over top photo, under center photo, over bottom photo and through bottom holes. Attach yarn to back side of page. To create three-layer tag, copy crocheting instructions onto tan paper and cut into three tags. Reinforce tag with green hole reinforcement. Thread tan crocheted chain through tag and attach to page. Adhere hook to page.

MaryJo Regier, Memory Makers Books

Supplies Green patterned paper (Design Originals); green stamping ink; tan cardstock
Found Objects Crochet hook; crochet chain-stitch samples; chain-stitch instructions; hole reinforcement

A Boy and a Pony

STRETCH ELASTIC'S USE WITH STAMPING

Searching her mother-in-law's sewing kit, Ramona discovered fitting page embellishments for a layout featuring a photo of her husband as a young boy. Attach snap and buttons to page. Stamp piece of elastic using brown stamping ink then staple elastic to page.

Ramona Greenspan, Yorktown Heights, New York

Supplies Patterned paper (DMD); letter stamps (Hero Arts); brown stamping ink; dark brown and brown cardstocks
Found Objects Buttons; snap; elastic; twine; staples

On the Rocks

CREATE A DIMENSIONAL ROCK RIVERBED

Using handpicked and hand-polished rocks from her mom's rock collection, Jenny made a compelling layout featuring her son, Jason. Using real rocks and steppingstone patterned paper, she continued the image of the riverbed in the photo into the riverbed on her layout. Mount cardstock on sturdy cardboard. Add patterned paper. Add steppingstone patterned paper to lower right corner. Silhouette crop rocks from remaining paper and adhere to layout using foam tape. Mat photos and adhere to layout. Using a strong adhesive, add polished rocks, carved stones and dried grass. Punch out frogs from green paper, bend frog legs to add dimension.

Jenny Moore Lowe, Lafayette, Colorado

Supplies Almond-crinkle patterned paper (Karen Foster Design); steppingstone patterned paper (Design Originals); letter stickers (Creative Imaginations); frog punch (McGill); brown and green cardstocks
Found Objects Polished rocks; engraved stones; dried grass

Jack

DANGLE A TITLE WITH RIBBON AND SAFETY PIN

Vanessa tells a colorful story about Earl and Merle, the names she gave her son's first two teeth. To reinforce the theme, she used colorful found accents on her page. Ink edges of stamped tag. Thread brightly colored ribbon though tag hole and wrap around page. Accent tag with green safety pin.

Vanessa Spady, Virginia Beach, Virginia

Supplies Green patterned papers (Karen Foster Design, Wordsworth); letter stamps (PSX Design); letter stickers (Wordsworth); green and brown stamping inks; photo corners; green cardstock
Found Objects Safety pin; ribbon

Sisters

CREATE BUTTON CLOSURE
FOR HIDDEN JOURNALING

Candi wrote a heartfelt note to her two nieces (tucked in a hidden journaling panel behind smaller photo) and found an inexpensive way to make a closure for her journaling with two buttons and embroidery floss. Print journaling on an 8½ x 11" piece of cream cardstock. Trim cardstock to 3½ x 10". Make fold ¼" above center line. Fold card then ink edges. Mount photo on front. Sew one button on front of card and sew another button inside. Use embroidery floss to close card. To hang green tag, thread blue ribbon through tag hole and attach ribbon to backside.

Candi Gershon, Fishers, Indiana

Supplies Striped patterned paper (Making Memories); letter stickers (Doodlebug Design); heart stamp (Stampin' Up!); brown stamping ink; cream and light green cardstocks
Found Objects Buttons; blue ribbon; white embroidery floss

Joe

BUILD MASCULINE PAGE WITH SEWING SUPPLIES

While searching for a safety pin, Sandra found a plethora of treasures at the bottom of her sewing basket for this manly page. She used all of them on her page featuring her husband, a mechanical engineer, and the incredible storage area he built for her. Use pinking shears to cut patterned paper for page accent. To create title, using black embroidery floss, stitch letters on red squares, mat onto black squares then adhere Velcro to back. Attach squares to Velcro strip. Attach glossary from McCall's pattern to page using black snaps. Run tracing wheel over layout to add texture. Accent page with rickrack, hat pin, safety pin, heart charm, red embroidery floss, needle threader and hook-and-eye fastener.

Sandra Blazek, Franksville, Wisconsin

Supplies Tan, red and black cardstocks; tape measure patterned paper (K & Company)
Found Objects Hat pin; needle threader; Velcro; tracing wheel; red and black embroidery floss; heart charm; black and silver snaps; red rickrack; McCall's pattern glossary; pinking shears; hook-and-eye fastener

Kyoto, Japan

TURN FABRIC SWATCHES INTO A DECORATIVE BORDER

When Joanna found fabric swatches with an Asian design, she knew they would complement the photos her husband took in Kyoto, Japan. Use white embroidery floss to hand stitch title onto black fabric. Wrap fabric around page to create 2½" black border. Layer with pink rickrack. Place 2½" strip of gold fabric on page; layer with black rickrack. Accent border with safety pin.

Joanna Bolick, Fletcher, North Carolina

Supplies Green cardstock
Found Objects Black and gold fabric; pink and black rickrack; white embroidery floss; safety pin

Always in Style

CREATE BULLETIN BOARD WITH RIBBON AND QUILTER'S TACKS

Inspired by photos of her niece, Arlen created a beautiful bulletin board on her page to display them. To create bulletin board, mount photos on cork-like patterned paper then add ribbon in a crisscross fashion, wrapping ends around the back. Mat bulletin board with pink cardstock and sew along edges to secure ribbon. Use foam tape to add quilter's tacks to bulletin board and tag. To mount focal photo, sew two hooks over strip of lace ribbon. Sew two eyes on photo mat. Hook pieces together. Accent page with small silk flowers and quilter's pins.

Arlen Schwarz, Virden, Illinois

Supplies Rose-crackle patterned paper (Making Memories); cork patterned paper (Karen Foster Design); letter stamps (Hero Arts, Making Memories, PSX Design); black stamping ink; pink cardstock

Found Objects Lace and red ribbons; large hooks and eyes; silk flowers; quilter's tacks; quilter's pins; safety pin

Little Girl Blue

ROUND UP LEATHER FRINGE AND WESTERN CONCHO

For a page featuring her daughter dressed as a cowgirl, Diana found fitting page accents in her sewing room. Mount 5½ x 10½" strip of brown checked paper to background paper. Accent bottom edge with leather fringe and nailheads. To make alphabet patterned paper resemble a page torn from a book, spray patterned paper with water and crumple. Unfold paper, lay flat then lightly rub ink pad directly onto creases. Adhere to page. Add western concho to tag. Thread leather ties through eyelets.

Diana Hudson, Bakersfield, California

Supplies Weathered-wood blue patterned paper (Karen Foster Design); alphabet patterned paper (Design Originals); brown checked patterned paper (Bo-Bunny Press); brown stamping ink

Found Objects Leather fringe; leather ties; nailheads; western concho accent from dress; eyelets

What One Loves in Childhood

RECAPTURE CHILDHOOD WITH QUILT SQUARES AND NEEDLEWORK

Jan created this page to reflect her love of handiwork that was passed down to her from her mother and grandmother. She even included a gingham block she designed in high school and quilt squares pieced by her grandmother. Mount quilt squares and needlework on cardstock. Layer with patterned paper, journaling block and photos. Place label holder over old photo. Accent current photo with rusted filigree corners. Use heart charm to replace the word "heart" in quote.

Jan Hicks, Arnold, Maryland

Supplies Brown and orange patterned paper (Wordsworth); stickers (Creative Imaginations); title quote (by MaryJo Putney from message board at TheGifted Note.com); brown and black stamping inks; brown and yellow cardstocks
Found Objects Quilt squares; needlework; label holder; rusted filigree decorative corners; charms; jewelry; nailheads; paper clips

Edward and Maud

CREATE HERITAGE ACCENTS WITH FLOSS AND CANDY WRAPPERS

While organizing her assortment of embroidery floss, Rozanne discovered striking vintage paper: the embroidery floss wrappers. The black and gold from the wrappers influenced the color scheme for her heritage page. Hand paint background paper with acrylic paint. Decoupage paper frame with paper wrappers from embroidery floss. Print heritage photo on canvas and add to frame. To create title, cut out squares of gold ribbon, stamp with black ink and adhere to page. Print journaling on transparency, lightly color with acrylic paint and mount on gold candy wrappers. Accent page with black ribbon and decorative fringe.

Rozanne Paxman, West Jordan, Utah

Supplies Letter stamps (Stamp Craft); black stamping ink; black cardstock; photo canvas; vellum
Found Objects Acrylic paint; handmade paper frame; embroidery floss wrappers; candy wrappers; gold and black ribbon; transparency; fringe

Mackenzie Ann Melzer

ADD A DAINTY TOUCH WITH LACE AND PEARLS

To highlight the sepia-toned photo of her daughter, Heather wrapped it like a gift using ribbon, pearls and buttons from her sewing kit. Mount photo on brown cardstock then wrap lace ribbon and pearl strand around top left and bottom right corners. Add buttons. To create page corners, fold silk ribbon around corners of background paper.

Heather Melzer, Yorkville, Illinois

Supplies Cream patterned paper (Anna Griffin); brown cardstock
Found Objects Lace ribbon; pearl strand; buttons; silk ribbon

Pretending to Knit

INCORPORATE BUTTONS INTO BACKGROUND DESIGN

Melanie used items from her sewing kit to enhance a layout about her genuine effort to learn how to knit. Sew buttons to flower centers on floral patterned paper. Stamp large metal-rimmed square tag. Punch holes through sides of tag. Punch adjacent holes through background paper. Loop ribbon through holes in crisscross fashion to attach tag. Add straight pin to tag. Underline title with ribbon.

Melanie Bauer, Columbia, Missouri
Photos: Kathy Bauer, Mountain Home, Arkansas

Supplies Floral and striped patterned papers (Chatterbox); letter stickers (EK Success); letter stamps (Ma Vinci's Reliquary); large metal-rimmed square tag (Making Memories); olive green stamping ink; olive green and brown cardstocks
Found Objects Buttons; silk ribbon; straight pin

Chills and Thrills

FIND A NEW USE FOR A PRETTY GIFT BAG

Using the handles, paper and snow-flakes from one gift bag, Denise found a resourceful way to create a winter page that sparkles. To create background paper, dab purple cardstock with washcloth moistened with bleach. Use patterned paper from gift bag as a secondary background. To mute pattern on gift bag, decoupage paper with crumbled tissue paper and mount. Attach top button with foam tape. Add eyelets to top corners of focal photo. Use handle from gift bag to hang focal photo on top button. Print title on transparency and adhere to fabric remnants on page. Accent page with buttons, rickrack and snowflakes cut from gift bag.

Denise Tucker, Versailles, Indiana

Supplies Purple cardstock; foam tape; eyelets
Found Objects Bleach; paper from gift bag; tissue paper; buttons; gift bag handles; silver snowflakes from gift bag; transparency; fabric remnants; purple rickrack

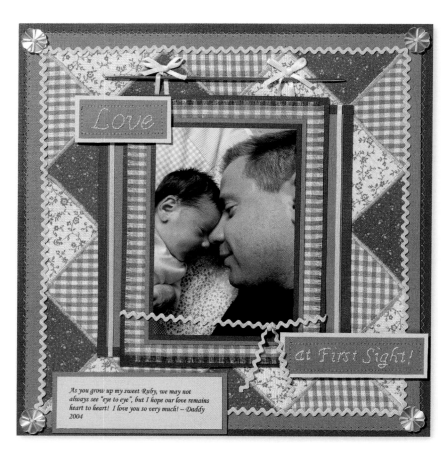

Love at First Sight

TRANSFORM FABRIC SCRAPS INTO DECORATIVE BACKGROUND

Inspired by the quilt in the photo, Andrea created an elaborate frame by using fabric scraps and consulting her quilting books. To create background, add fusible web-bing to fabric scraps then cut scraps into triangles. Position scraps to create a 1¾" mat border on cardstock. Remove paper backing. Iron each shape to keep it in place. Use zigzag stitch on machine to sew between shapes. Create mat for photo by layering various papers and fabric. Accent mat with pink ribbon and pink rickrack. Adhere mat to fabric frame. For title, hand stitch letters onto cardstock and adhere to page using foam tape. Attach knitting needle to page and accent with bows. Sew white button on each corner of the page using pink embroidery floss.

Andrea Lyn Vetten-Marley, Aurora, Colorado

Supplies Dark purple, light purple and purple cardstocks; foam tape
Found Objects Fabric scraps; fusible webbing; pink ribbon; pink rickrack; pink embroidery floss; knitting needle; buttons

Sand Artist

EMBELLISH PAGE WITH CRAFT SAND

Denise created a lovely and vibrant page showcasing her 4-year-old daughter, the sand artist. To create sand flowers, hand cut stems and leaves from adhesive paper then cover with sand. Punch flowers from adhesive paper using a daisy punch and a small flower punch then cover with sand. Mount decorative shapes on page. Accent title and pullout tag with sand flowers.

Denise Tucker, Versailles, Indiana

Supplies Black and pink cardstocks; daisy and small flower punch (Carl, EK Success)
Found Objects Colored craft sand

Snow Baby

MIMIC SNOW WITH DRYER SHEETS

When Marianne noticed that the dryer sheet came out of the dryer looking like powdery snow—light and fluffy—she knew it would make a wonderful background for a winter layout showcasing her niece in her new snow outfit. Adhere dryer sheets to light pink cardstock; place bright pink cardstock on top. Tear cardstock to reveal dryer sheets underneath. Mount cardstock and reinforce edges with turquoise thread and blanket stitch. Mount photos. Use white brads to accent photo corners. Tie strip of dryer sheet around tag.

Marianne Dobbs, Alpena, Michigan
Photos: Christina Poston, Baring, Missouri

Supplies Title and tag (Sizzix); punches (EK Success, Punch Bunch); letter stamps and dot stickers (Stampendous); bright pink and light pink cardstocks
Found Objects Dryer sheets; turquoise thread; white brads

Faux Leather Accents

Heat a brown foam sheet with a heat-embossing gun and stamp into the foam to create leather-like page accents. Silhouette crop the accents or crop into the shape of a tag, if desired. Rub faux leather images with chalk or ink to add dimension.

Frugal Bonus Idea #14

A Flair for Sewing

FIND INSPIRATION FROM A NEW PAIR OF JEANS

When Pamela saw the tag on her daughter's new "flare" jeans, she got a brilliant idea for a page featuring her home studio. Pamela's tailoring expertise came in handy when it was time to make tucks, insert a zipper and sew a zigzag border. Make decorative border using denim, embroidery floss and zigzag stitch. Mat focal photo on frayed piece of denim reinforced with stitching and accent corners with safety pins. To create large V-shaped denim pocket, make 10 tucks, insert zipper and sew onto page. Accent pocket with label plate. Sew stamped word blocks onto layout. Alter words on tag to create title and attach to page with ribbon and safety pin.

Pamela James, Ventura, California

Supplies Stamped patterned paper (Club Scrap); lowercase letter stamps (PSX Design); uppercase letter stamps (Colorbök); black stamping ink

Found Objects Denim scrap; embroidery floss; thread; label plate; brads; tag from jeans; ribbon; safety pin

I'll Forever Cherish your

Butterfly Kisses

ADD SOFTNESS WITH LACE, RIBBON AND BUTTERFLIES

Inspired by Bob Carlisle's song, Andrea created an intricate layout showcasing her daughter, Brianna. To create page border, attach pink lace ribbon to cardstock. To create title block, stitch words on purple paper using pink embroidery floss; mat and mount on page above and below miniature dress. Mat title and mount with foam tape. To create mini blinds, accordion-fold paper and stitch folds together. Position blinds above photo and attach chain-stitched crocheted drawstring. Wrap drawstring around brad. To create decorative white frosting on journaling block, use cake decorating bag filled with white modeling paste. Make butterflies using butterfly punch and butterfly die-cut. Dry emboss butterflies then pierce them to make them look lacey. Add to layout with butterfly appliqués.

Andrea Lyn Vetten-Marley, Aurora, Colorado

Supplies Pink floral patterned paper (Colorbök); butterfly punches (Emagination Crafts, McGill); butterfly die cut (Ellison); stencil (Dreamweaver); dress (source unknown); pink striped paper; purple paper; foam tape; light green and purple cardstocks
Found Objects Pink lace; white lace; green ribbon; pink and purple embroidery floss; modeling paste and cake decorating bag; butterfly appliqués

Granny

STRENGTHEN MEMORIES WITH VINTAGE SEWING SUPPLIES

Elizabeth found an amazing supply of vintage embellishments in one spot: Granny's old sewing kit. Not only do these embellishments look chic today, they remind Elizabeth of her talented seamstress grandmother. Elizabeth created the striking background paper by taking a photo of a quilt her Granny made and enlarging it to 12 x 18" to span across her layout. To create accent paper on left page, copy inside of vintage sewing needle packaging and adhere to page. Attach outside of vintage sewing needle packaging to right page. Use ribbon to attach painted label holder. Accent title with pin. To create hidden journaling on right page, print text and trim paper to 7 x 11" and fold into three sections. Punch holes into the ends of an 8" strip of tape measure. Wrap around journaling and adhere to page. Thread ribbon through eyelets to close journaling. Accent page with vintage ads, snaps and needle packaging.

Elizabeth Ruuska, Rensselaer, Indiana
Photo: Olan Mills, Dayton, Ohio

Supplies Gingham patterned paper (Close To My Heart); letter stamps (PSX Design); rub-on statements (Making Memories); black stamping ink
Found Objects Vintage needle and snap packaging; vintage ads; tape measure; ribbon; label holder; pin; buttons; eyelets

Frugal Bonus Idea #15

Faux Wax Seals

Drip a small puddle of colored hot glue from a glue gun onto paper and press a stamp into the glue for five minutes to make a faux wax seal.

Patterned With You in Mind

DISCOVER VINTAGE PATTERN IN THE SEWING ROOM

For a page about her daughter learning to sew, Carol created a vintage layout using sewing supplies and an old pattern of her mother's. Adhere packaging from old pattern to sewing pattern background paper. Adhere an 8½" zipper, 12" strip of tape measure, rickrack and lace for added detail. Age items with chalk. To create tag, adhere fabric swatches to tag and add title created with label maker. Set snap in tag hole. Use threaded needle to attach vintage needle packaging. Mount photo with safety pin. Accent page with buttons and label from spool of thread.

Carol Darilek, Austin, Texas

Supplies Sewing pattern patterned paper (Li'l Davis Designs); chalk
Found Objects Vintage pattern and needle packaging; label maker; needle; thread; buttons; thread spool label; tape measure; zipper; rickrack; lace for hemming; straight pins; safety pin

First Day of School

CREATE DECORATIVE BORDERS WITH STITCHING AND FIBERS

Summer brought out the red lunch box in the photo using red thread, red ribbon and red stamping ink. Ink edges of tan cardstock with red ink. Use red thread and zigzag stitch to attach 5½ x 11" strip of striped vellum to page. Mount photo onto crumbled red paper mat using white paper clips. Create border by wrapping red ribbon, hemp cord, and white and blue fibers around page, securing on backside with tape. Accent decorative border with stamped tags and white paper clips. Accent journaling block with hemp cord and white paper clip. Stamp date.

Summer Ford, San Antonio, Texas

Supplies Striped vellum (SEI); large letter stamps (Stampin' Up!); small letter stamps (Hero Arts); red stamping ink; tan and red cardstocks
Found Objects Red ribbon; red thread; hemp cord; blue and white fringe; paper clips; date stamp

SOMETIMES IT IS
THE SIMPLEST JOYS
THAT BRING
THE HEART ITS
SWEETEST PLEASURES

Cole in a box 10.13.03

A P T E R 5

Garage & Workshop

Last, but not least, we arrive at the garage and workshop—the less-esteemed but highly utilitarian chambers of dust, must and rust and long-forgotten treasures. While many garages pull double-duty as hobby workshops—complete with the comforts of air, light, heat and ventilation—most garages are filled with ubiquitous items saved for "one of these days." Where your garage and workshop are concerned, toss open those workbenches, toolboxes and nut-and-bolt drawers and proclaim today the day!

Rescue newsprint and corrugated cardboard from your recycling bins. Retrieve all those leftover paint and laminate chips, car restoration parts and drywall tape. Recover clay-pot shards, chicken wire and screen fragments and empty garden seed packets from the trash. Stake your claim on fishing tackle, sandpaper and various fasteners of all types and shapes—all in the name of scrapbooking.

One hour of tinkering and toiling in your garage and workshop will reward you in trinkets that add depth and texture to scrapbook pages. So turn that garage and workspace upside down in pursuit of found items and whatever you find, you're sure to have a riveting experience!

Ètienne

CONVERT SMALL HARDWARE FINDS INTO PAGE ACCENTS

Caroline wrote a lovely poem to her 4-year-old son and attached it to her page with hinges. She held the poem in place with a lever from an old picture frame. It opens up to reveal hidden journaling. The label holder came from an old storage box. Print journaling in red on white paper, trim to 10 x 4" and tear left edge. Chalk all edges. Mount journaling on red background paper with hinges and eyelets. Attach lever to hold journaling in place. Behind journaling block, adhere hidden journaling. Attach label holder displaying stamped name.

Caroline Huot, Laval, Quebec, Canada
Photo: Daniel Huot, Montreal, Quebec, Canada

Supplies Green patterned paper (Anna Griffin); letter stamps (Trodat); white stamping ink; chalk; eyelets; red and white cardstocks
Found Objects Hinges; label holder; picture frame lever; brads

Mon Petit Coquin

Tu as déjà soufflé tes quatre bougies
Tu es déjà rendu si grand
Tu bouge sans cesse, t'es plein de vie
Je voudrais arrêter le temps...

Dire qu'il n'y a que quelque temps
Tu n'étais qu'un minuscule paquet muet
Tu préférais de loin tes parents
À n'importe quel dispendieux jouet

Tes intérêts semblent sans fin
Sports, livres, ordinateurs, musique, dessin
T'es rendu tellement intelligent
Tu nous poses des questions constamment

Tu as ton caractère bien à toi
Les bibittes, les chiens, ça te met en effroi
Un peu timide, mais très affectueux
En tant que fils, je ne peux demander mieux

Bientôt, tu deviendras le grand frère
J'en ressens une anxiété douce-amère
J'ai peur que tu en veuilles, à moi ou à lui,
De ne plus être seul, de ne plus être petit

Sache, mon coquin, que toujours, dans mon cœur
Tu seras la raison de mon bonheur
Et même quand tu seras grand
Je t'aimerai toujours autant

Maman, xxx
9 mai 1999

ÉTIENNE 4½ANS

Found Treasures From the Garage & Workshop

Aquarium gravel	Fishing tackle	Newspaper
Carpet samples	Fishing tackle labels	Nuts and bolts
Chicken wire	Garden seeds and packets	Old screens
Clay pot fragments	Gardening moss or soil	Paint chips
Copper and aluminum sheeting	Gaskets	Rivets
Corrugated cardboard	Hinges	Sand
Countertop laminate chips	Keys	Sandpaper
Dog tags	Leftover car restoration parts	Shells
Dried plant and flower sprigs	License plates	Small coils
Drywall tape	Linoleum and tile samples	Thin rope
Electrical tape	Nail and screw heads	Toggle bolts
Electrical wire	Nails	Washers

Team Effort

MAKE A POWERFUL STATEMENT WITH A LICENSE PLATE

Becky was browsing through a local antique shop when she found a license plate with her son's jersey number on it. Coincidently, the colors of the plate matched his school's colors. She used numbers from the license plate to create a handsome sports layout. Accent black cardstock with black and white patterned paper. Cut number from license plate and attach to page with brad. Cut two 1 x 8" strips from yellow paper. Use black ink to ink edges and adhere to page. Using a black marker, color label holders. Place label plates over stamped title and attach to layout with brads.

Becky Novacek, Fremont, Nebraska

Supplies Black and white patterned paper (7 Gypsies); letter stamps (PSX Design); black stamping ink; black marker; black and yellow cardstocks
Found Objects License plate; label holders; brads

My Tools

FORM ALPHABET LETTERS
WITH WORKSHOP FASTENERS

Using screws, washers and wire, Stephanie created a riveting layout featuring her son Jacob outfitted in his work overalls and playing at his tool bench. To create title block, use washers for the "o" letters, make the letter "s" with braided wire and use various sizes and colors of screws to form the straight-edged letters. Sew all items to red mat using a thin wire. Mount red mat on blue mat using foam tape. Use eyelets to attach title blocks to page.

Stephanie Stallcup, Ben Wheeler, Texas

Supplies Yellow tool patterned paper (source unknown); vellum; tool die cuts (Westrim); eyelets; red and blue cardstocks
Found Objects Screws; washers; braided wire

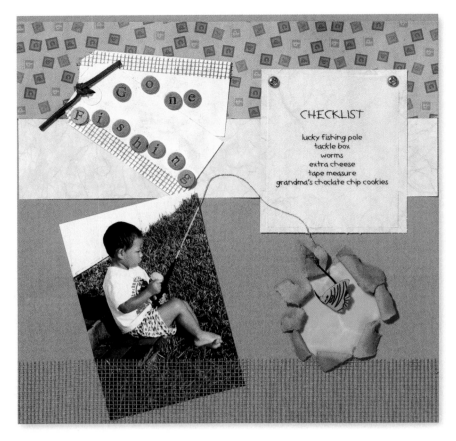

Gone Fishing

ADD A HOOK TO A FISHING HOLE

For a page featuring her grandson fishing at the lake, Diane created a fishing hole on her page and added one of Grandpa's fishing hooks to bring the photo to life. Tear hole in background paper to make fishing hole. Place piece of water-patterned vellum behind fishing hole. Adhere gold thread, fishing hook and fish button to page. Attach journaling block with screw eyelets. Create 2" wide border on bottom of page using mesh. Accent title tag with drywall tape.

Diane Sanchez, Melbourne, Florida
Photo: Photography by Chez, Melbourne, Florida

Supplies Patterned paper (EK Success); water-like vellum (Provo Craft); letters and screw eyelets (Making Memories); orange cardstock
Found Objects Drywall tape; screw heads; fish hook; fish button; gold thread

I Pick This One

STAMP TITLE ON SANDPAPER

To create an intriguing texture for her fall layout featuring her son at the pumpkin patch, Kimberly bravely printed her title on sandpaper and used pumpkin seeds for embellishments. To avoid damaging the printer cartridge, we recommend stamping title onto sandpaper. To achieve a rustic look, sand striped patterned paper and adhere to orange background paper. Stamp title on fine sandpaper, tear bottom edge of sandpaper and mount on layout over striped paper. Mount pumpkin seeds on small black squares and attach to page next to each journaling block.

Kimberly DeLong, Fremont, Michigan

Supplies Striped patterned paper (Scrapbook Wizard); label patterned paper (Rusty Pickle); orange and black cardstocks
Found Objects Sandpaper; pumpkin seeds

A Life's Work

ADD REALISM WITH RIG SET AND HOOK

Jane found an innovative embellishment for her fishing layout in her husband's tackle box: a panfish and crappie rig set. Ink edges of tan background paper with cranberry ink to give page an outdoorsy look. Create two descriptive borders with label maker to go across top and bottom of page. Ink edges of photo. Attach rig set and hook to page.

Jane Swanson, Janesville, Wisconsin

Supplies Patterned paper (Club Scrap); tags and triangles (Patchwork Paper Design); cranberry stamping ink
Found Objects Panfish and crappie rig set and hook; label maker

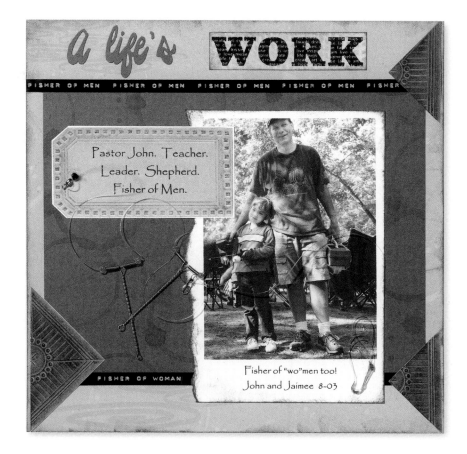

Timeless Beauty

USE HANDS FROM CLOCK FOR EVERLASTING APPEAL

To emphasize the theme of her simple yet compelling layout, Suzy made a stylized clock. To make clock, cut a 7" circle from time-definition patterned paper and mount on background paper. Attach clock hands to center of circle. Accent top right corner with additional clock hand. Attach metal lever to bottom left corner to draw attention to poem on transparency.

Suzy West, Fremont, California

Supplies Time-definition patterned paper (Carolee's Creations); title letter stickers (Me & My Big Ideas); rust cardstock
Found Objects Clock hands; metal lever; transparency

Frugal Bonus Idea #16

Faux Metal or Wood Frames

Rip strips of masking tape into small pieces. Overlap and adhere tape pieces randomly all over frame surface and trim away any excess overlap from frame's edges. Rub chalk, metallic rub-ons or ink over the surface of tape to add texture and depth. If desired, clear emboss frame with ultra thick embossing powder to add luster.

Revell '70 Plymouth Roadrunner

FRAME PHOTOS WITH PIECES FROM A MODEL CAR KIT

Using leftover pieces from her son's model car kit, MaryJo ingeniously created frames to showcase photos of her son Dylan building and painting a model car. A closer look at her page reveals stunning background paper she created using instructions from the model car kit. To create model car transparency, copy instructions from the model car kit onto an 8½ x 11" transparency. Print journaling block on the same transparency and adhere to page. For title block, use packaging label from kit. Frame photos using leftover pieces and parts from model car kit. Silhouette small photos of paint and model glue containers and adhere to page. Use label maker to create date strip and display on model car part.

MaryJo Regier, Memory Makers Books

Supplies Woven patterned paper (Karen Foster Design); black cardstock
Found Objects Model car packaging; transparency; leftover pieces and parts from model car kit; label maker

The Vettens Don't Waste Time...

ADD REALISM WITH FISHING NET, STRINGERS AND FLIES

Andrea captured the excitement of trout fishing in a "top secret location" by using a real fishing net, large metal stringers and a handful of fishing flies. Mount 11½ x 11½" light brown paper on 12 x 12" dark brown paper. Attach net, wrapping excess around back of page. Tear out title on tan paper then ink edges with ginger stamping ink and adhere to page. Attach flies to pieces of torn tan paper with inked edges. Place flies, stringers, swivels and vintage hook box in netting.

Andrea Lyn Vetten-Marley, Aurora, Colorado

Supplies Dark brown, light brown and tan cardstocks; ginger stamping ink
Found Objects Fishing net; fishing flies, fishing stringers; fishing swivels; vintage hook box

Very First Pony Ride

ADD KICK TO A TITLE WITH JUTE STRING

Heather gave her layout a snappy western look by making a textured title out of jute string. Adhere 6 x 12" piece of patterned paper to brown background paper. To create title, adhere metal letters then outline "pony ride" title with pencil. Adhere jute string over pencil lines using thin line of liquid glue. Use twine and eyelets to attach journaling to layout.

Heather Melzer, Yorkville, Illinois

Supplies Brown cardstock; daisy patterned paper (source unknown); metal letters (Making Memories); eyelets
Found Objects Jute string; twine

Rustic Life

ACHIEVE A HISTORIC LOOK WITH RUSTY OBJECTS

For a page featuring the 1870s loft Trisha and her husband renovated, Trisha gathered up rusty objects—gems in her eyes—that she found either in her garage or while on a walk. For a page accent, she used a crystal from an old chandelier. On the rolled-up note in the small bottle, she wrote about the building's history. To make the background paper, she used an antique stencil from a dry goods sack that her husband found in a flour mill warehouse. Using stencil, create lettering on light yellow cardstock with a dry brush and brown acrylic paint. Ink edges of cardstock and photo with brown stamping ink. Adhere photo to page and accent corners with mirror rosettes. Use strong adhesive to attach rusty objects to page. Add magnetic poetry words to rusty objects. Age journaling block with walnut ink, roll up and insert into small brown bottle. Add washers, souvenir pen, ribbon, key and crystal from chandelier.

Trisha McCarty-Luedke, Memory Makers *magazine*

Supplies Light yellow cardstock; brown stamping ink; walnut ink
Found Objects Antique stencil; brown acrylic paint; small brown bottle; crystal from chandelier; wire; mirror rosettes; rusty metal scraps and watch face; rusty bottle cap and washers; souvenir pen; ribbon; key

Cool Wheels

INCORPORATE PAINT CHIPS WITH FASTENERS

A handful of page accents from the garage became fitting embellishments for Tracy's page about her son's first "big boy" bike. Mat focal photo and mount on page. Attach secondary photo to page using a hinge and brads. Adhere rubber ring on right side of photo to serve as handle for hidden journaling behind photo. Use paint chip for page accent. Adhere metal letter on paint chip. Use two washers for the letter "o" in the word "cool." Draw attention to the word "boy" in definition with washer.

Tracy Clements, Smithville, Ontario, Canada

Supplies Striped patterned paper (Chatterbox); license plate patterned paper (DMD); definition paper (Carolee's Creations); metal letters (Making Memories); "a" sticker (Sticker Studio); dime, postage stamp and passport stickers (Karen Foster Design); light green and green cardstocks
Found Objects Washers; hinges; paint chip; rubber ring

One can never consent to creep
when one feels an impulse to soar.
— Helen Keller

Soar

RAISE PHOTO USING WASHERS AND RIBBON

For a layout featuring her daughter running through the sprinklers, Vanessa created the illusion of the photo soaring off the page using washers, ribbon and foam tape. To create raised border on background paper, cut ¼" frame from patterned paper and mount on matching background paper using foam tape. To create raised focal photo, mat photo with patterned paper, add washers to mat and mount on page using foam tape. Thread ribbon through washers and tie to frame. Accent frame with ribbon.

Vanessa Spady, Virginia Beach, Virginia

Supplies Patterned paper (Provo Craft); quote (DieCuts With a View); lettering template (Wordsworth); cocoa stamping ink; foam tape
Found Objects Washers; ribbon

We're Wired

FIND A NEW USE FOR ELECTRICAL ODDS AND ENDS

For a page featuring her boys hooked up for EEGs, electrical items from the garage became ideal embellishments for Michelle's page. To create page border, adhere white and blue electrical tape to edges of background paper. Use the same tape to create first word in title. To create the word "wired," shape letters out of wire and use fishing line to attach letters to squares cut from window screen. Attach picture hangers to photo using screws. Loop wire through picture hangers. Mount photo on page with foam tape. Accent page with computer chips; electrodes and wire.

Michelle Pendleton, Colorado Springs, Colorado

Supplies Yellow and light yellow cardstocks
Found Objects Window screen; fishing line; white and blue electrical tape; screws; picture hangers; computer chips; electrodes; electrical wire

WE'RE WIRED

Adam and Luke enjoy being hooked up to many wires during their EEGs. They hold mirrors and watch the electrodes being applied to their scalp. The boys are sleep deprived for the testing and easily fall asleep in the big comfy chairs. Since they were diagnosed with epilepsy when they were four years old they have become model patients when it comes to getting all wired up.
Adam (top) and Luke (bottom)
November 21, 2000

Colt's Camaro

ENHANCE STORY WITH CAR PARTS AND CAR PUTTY

MaryJo tells an exciting and detailed story about the two-year restoration project on her son's Camaro and the family's love affair with American "muscle cars." To bring the story to life, she gathered leftover items from the restoration project for her page. Create border using strips of aluminum body repair tape. Adhere Chevrolet decal over printed title. Download Camaro logo from Internet, trace with watermark ink or watermark pen and emboss with glitter embossing powder. Apply car body putty to journaling block. Use label maker to make "before" and "after" captions. Attach grinder disk to page. Accent page with fuses, nuts, electrical wire and wiper linkage bracket.

MaryJo Regier, Memory Makers Books

Supplies Watermark ink (Tsukineko) or watermark pen; blue and cream cardstocks; glitter embossing powder; foam tape
Found Objects Aluminum body repair tape; fuses; nuts; electrical wire; wiper linkage bracket; grinder disk; car body putty; Chevrolet decal; label maker

Frugal Bonus Idea #17

Aging Photos

Rub sandpaper or steel wool across a photo surface or around its edges to distress and age the photo.

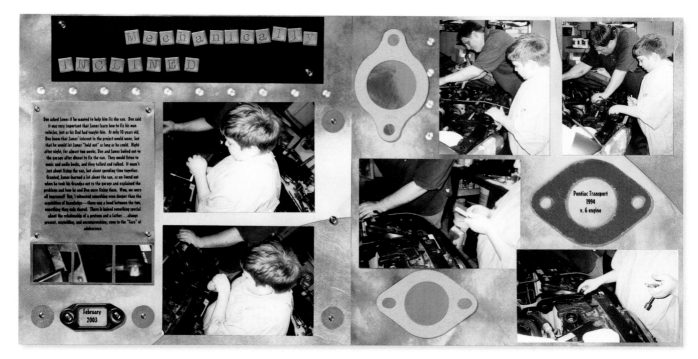

Mechanically Inclined

USE VEHICLE GASKETS AS A DESIGN ELEMENT

For a page about a father and son working together to fix a car, Pam found a compelling page embellishment in their workshop: gaskets. Use brads to attach title block, journaling block and label holder. Place silver paper under blue gaskets and adhere to page. Place transparency with car name under gray gasket and adhere to page. Display date in label holder. Accent page with metal circles and brads.

Pam Canavan, Clermont, Florida

Supplies Patterned paper (Paper Loft); letter stickers (All My Memories); silver paper and circles (ScrapTherapy Designs); black transparency
Found Objects Vehicle gaskets; label holder; transparency; brads

South Carolina

ADD TEXTURE WITH CARDBOARD

Dana drew inspiration for her beach layout from an assortment of items she found in her husband's shed including an old nylon screen, a handful of seashells and a dog tag from 1998. Using white acrylic paint, paint a 5 x 10½" piece of screen and attach to page. To create frame, paint a 5½ x 7½" piece of corrugated cardboard with white acrylic paint. Cut out center to create a 1¼" wide frame. Tie candlestick wick around lower right section of frame. Adhere tape measure strip to right edge of frame. Hang dog tag to metal ring on tape measure. Create bottom border using measuring tape. Mat smaller photos on painted corrugated cardboard. Accent page with seashells.

Dana Swords, Fredericksburg, Virginia

Supplies Letter stamps (All Night Media); black stamping ink; dark blue, light blue and brown cardstocks
Found Objects Corrugated cardboard; white acrylic paint; nylon screen; seashells; tape measure; candle wicking; dog tag

The Last Catch of the Day

SEARCH TACKLE BOX FOR PAGE EMBELLISHMENTS

To capture the passion her son Anthony has for fishing, Paula rummaged through his tackle box and found a few great page embellishments. Attach title block using eyelets, fishing line and swivel. To create tag, use eyelets to attach vellum journaling block. Adhere fishing fly to tag. Tie green fiber that resembles pond weed to tag. Accent page with green fiber.

Paula Frances Jones, Caledon, Ontario, Canada

Supplies Purple patterned paper (Carolee's Creations); eyelets; blue cardstock
Found Objects Fishing line; fishing fly; fishing swivel; green fiber

Mom's Garden

RECYCLE EMPTY SEED PACKETS AND CHICKEN WIRE

Elizabeth brilliantly conveyed her passion for gardening with items from her garden workshop and descriptive journaling. She even transferred the words from her garden stake to make the title block using a colored pencil. To create page, sand empty packets of seeds to give them a worn look. Adhere torn sections to page, laying portions of packaging on top of one another. Continue to add layers using pieces from the newspaper featuring gardening news. Attach a 4 x 11" piece of chicken wire used for climbing plants. Use twine to attach title block. Mount photos on page, slipping center photo into corner of seed packet.

Elizabeth Ruuska, Rensselaer, Indiana

Supplies Light pink patterned paper (Paper Loft); colored pencils
Found Objects Chicken wire; seed packets; twine; transparency; garden stake

Finely Tuned

TRY WASHERS AS STENCILS TO CREATE PATTERNED PAPER

For a page showcasing her son tuning up his bike, Kelli created a striking page using her own background paper made with spray paint and washers. To create patterned paper, place different sizes of washers in a pattern on blue cardstock. Using washers as a stencil, spray cardstock with paint resembling stone. To create border, adhere a ¾" strip of drywall tape to a 1" strip of blue paper. Mount title on border. To attach journaling block, use picture hangers and chain. Use label maker to create subtitle. Accent page with large washers.

Kelli Noto, Centennial, Colorado

Supplies Die-cut letters (QuicKutz); blue cardstock
Found Objects Spray paint (Krylon); drywall tape; chain; washers; picture hangers; label maker

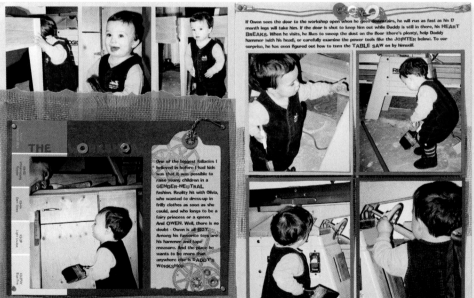

The Workshop

LOOK IN TOOL BOX FOR RIVETING PAGE ACCENTS

With a series of photos featuring her toddler in Daddy's workshop—Owen's favorite place to be—Mary-Catherine discovered an assortment of unique page accents in the same location. On left page, adhere torn vellum to background. Staple large pieces of wire screen over vellum. Attach paint chip to blue cardstock using brads. Use nut and bolt for the two letter "o's" in the title; use red stickers for remainder of title. Stamp tag with gear stamp. Thread wire and washers through tag hole and adhere to blue paper. Mount blue paper on page with brads. To create top border on right page, thread bolts and washers through picture hanging wire. Attach wire to page using brads.

Mary-Catherine Kropinski, Coquitlam, British Columbia, Canada

Supplies Light and dark blue cardstocks; light blue vellum (source unknown); stickers (Provo Craft); gear stamp (JudiKins); brown stamping ink
Found Objects Wire screen; paint chip; picture hanger wire; washers; brads

Additional Instructions & Credits

Page 1

JUNK

Miscellaneous items from a drawer in Angie's kitchen reveal small details about each member of her family. She displays them separately on paper shapes to highlight the importance of each. Trim a rectangle of gray paper and cover with white squares and rectangles. Adhere found objects to white cardstock.

Angie Head, Friendswood, Texas

Supplies Black, gray and white cardstocks
Found Objects Handwritten note; foreign coin; cork; button; mug charm; birthday candle; domino; plastic bone; die; padlock; metal chain; Lego piece; penny; barrette

Page 6

GERBRANDTS

A colorful photo of Michele's family was accented with coordinating fabric scraps. Layer drywall tape over blue cardstock background. Tear edges of yellow cardstock, layer over drywall tape and add flower image cut from a greeting card. Cut fabric into strips, fray edges and layer along edges of page. Adhere buttons to fabric, tying with thin fabric pieces. Cut title letters from red fabric to coordinate. Cut first letter of title using stencil and paint with red acrylic paint.

Supplies Letter die cuts (QuicKutz); blue and yellow cardstocks; vellum; embossing powder
Found Objects Drywall tape; buttons; fabric; greeting cards; stencil; acrylic paint

Page 12

THIS FACE

Joanna's page background was inspired by business-reply postcards that typically fall from magazines and end up on her kitchen floor. Gather several postcards and layer across black background. For fold-out journaling, write on pieces of recipe cards and adhere them to a strip of blue cardstock. Score and fold each end so they meet in the center. Crumple aluminum foil, flatten and adhere to one flap. Attach product-packaging closure to ends of each flap. Add packaging bar code and drink and food can tops. Attach a small refrigerator magnet to the bottom of the page.

Joanna Bolick, Fletcher, North Carolina

Supplies Red, black, blue and tan textured cardstocks (Bazzill)
Found Objects Business reply postcards; food-packaging closure; aluminum foil; bar code; sunflower magnet; recipe cards; drink and food can tops

Page 28

REPOSE

While in the process of building a new house, Joanna's bedroom contained a variety of wallpaper remnants. Trim wallpaper to cover black background; layer with photograph. Attach thin black strips across bottom of page and accent with gold token from a jewelry box. Remove back from butterfly earring and adhere over token.

Joanna Bolick, Fletcher, North Carolina

Supplies Black cardstock
Found Objects Wallpaper remnants; gold token; earring

Page 48

10 THINGS WE LOVE ABOUT YOU

A simple manila file folder, envelope and binder clips from Joanna's home office accent portraits of Joanna's son while keeping the focus on the pictures. Mount photos on manila envelope; attach envelope to file folder with foam tape. Add binder clips above photos and adhere all to black background. Type definitions on typewriter; tear out and adhere between photos. Print journaling, cut into strips and attach to bottom of envelope.

Joanna Bolick, Fletcher, North Carolina

Supplies Gray and black cardstocks; white paper; foam tape
Found Objects 9 x 12" envelope; file folder; binder clips; typewriter

Page 64

HANDMADE WITH LOVE

Mellette used various items from her sewing room to attach journaling on top of her photos. Using a needle and embroidery floss, hand stitch one word of title through tan patterned paper. Cut strip from sewing patterns and adhere to bottom of page. Line edges of title and pattern with ribbon. Print journaling on vellum, cut apart and attach to photographs with straight pins, safety pins, buttons and eyelets. Trim edges of small fabric piece with pinking shears, machine stitch ends, stamp name and adhere to photo with large safety pin.

Mellette Berezoski, Crosby, Texas

Supplies Tan patterned paper (Close To My Heart); red metal heart (Carolee's Creations); silver rose embellishment (Boutique Trims); letter stamps (PSX Design); black stamping ink
Found Objects Sewing pattern; fabric; thread; pinking shears; ribbon; embroidery floss; pins; eyelet; button

Page 80

COLE IN A BOX

A photo of Joanna's son in a cardboard box was best complemented with a cardboard backdrop, in addition to other items found in her garage. Cut out 11 x 11" square from cardboard box and tear away the top layer; set aside. Brush corrugated surface with white paint. Mount metal shelving strips on cardstock; layer cardboard over metal with black cardstock. Tape top layer of cardboard to cardstock in order to print journaling on it. Remove cardboard layer from cardstock and attach over corrugated surface with screws. Accent page with key, more screws and bottle top altered to represent subject's name.

Joanna Bolick, Fletcher, North Carolina

Supplies Black cardstock; red pen
Found Objects Cardboard box; paint; screws; metal shelving strips; bottle top; key; wire

Sources

While the majority of products used in this book were "found" items, the following companies manufacture scrapbook-related products featured in this book. Please check your local retailers to find these materials. In addition, we have made every attempt to properly credit the items mentioned in this book. We apologize to any company that we have listed incorrectly or if the sources were unknown, and we would appreciate hearing from you.

3M
(800) 364-3577
www.3M.com

7 Gypsies
(800) 588-6707
www.7gypsies.com

All My Memories
(888) 553-1998
www.allmymemories.com

All Night Media (see Plaid Enterprises)

American Crafts
(800) 879-5185
www.americancrafts.com

American Tag Company
(800) 223-3956
www.americantag.net

Amscan, Inc.
(800) 444-8887
www.amscan.com

Anna Griffin, Inc (wholesale only)
(888) 817-8170
www.annagriffin.com

Avery Dennison Corporation
(800) GO-AVERY
www.avery.com

Bazzill Basics Paper
(480) 558-8557
www.bazzillbasics.com

Bo-Bunny Press
(801) 771-0481
www.bobunny.com

Boutique Trims, Inc.
(248) 437-2017
www.boutiquetrims.com

CARL Mfg. USA, Inc.
(800) 257-4771
www.carl-products.com

Carolee's Creations®
(435) 563-1100
www.carolees.com

Chatterbox, Inc.
(208) 939-9133
www.chatterboxinc.com

Clearsnap, Inc.
(800) 448-4862
www.clearsnap.com

Close To My Heart®
(888) 655-6552
www.closetomyheart.com

Cloud 9 Design
(763) 493-0990
www.cloud9design.biz

Club Scrap™
(888) 634-9100
www.clubscrap.com

Colorbök™, Inc. (wholesale only)
(800) 366-4660
www.colorbok.com

Craf-T Products
(507) 235-3996
www.craf-tproducts.com

Creative Imaginations (wholesale only)
(800) 942-6487
www.cigift.com

C-Thru® Ruler Company, The (wholesale only)
(800) 243-8419
www.cthruruler.com

Current®, Inc.
(800) 848-2848
www.currentinc.com

Daisy D's Paper Company
(888) 601-8955
www.daisydspaper.com

Delta Technical Coatings, Inc.
(800) 423-4135
www.deltacrafts.com

Deluxe Designs
(480) 497-9005
www.deluxecuts.com

DeNami Design Rubber Stamps
(253) 437-1626
www.denamidesign.com

Design Originals
(800) 877-7820
www.d-originals.com

DieCuts with a View™
(877) 221-6107
www.dcwv.com

DMD Industries, Inc.
(800) 805-9890
www.dmdind.com

Doodlebug Design, Inc.™
(801) 966-9952
www.doodlebugdesignsinc.com

Dreamweaver Stencils
(909) 824-8343
www.dreamweaverstencils.com

Duro Decal Co.—no contact info available

EK Success™, Ltd. (wholesale only)
(800) 524-1349
www.eksuccess.com

Ellison® Craft & Design
(800) 253-2238
www.ellison.com

Emagination Crafts, Inc. (wholesale only)
(630) 833-9521
www.emaginationcrafts.com

Fiskars, Inc. (wholesale only)
(715) 842-2091
www.fiskars.com

Foofala
(402) 330-3208
www.foofala.com

Hero Arts® Rubber Stamps, Inc.
(wholesale only)
(800) 822-4376
www.heroarts.com

Hot Off The Press, Inc.
(800) 227-9595
www.paperpizazz.com

Impress Rubber Stamps
(206) 901-9101
www.impressrubberstamps.com

Inkadinkado® Rubber Stamps
(800) 888-4652
www.inkadinkado.com

It Takes Two®
(800) 331-9843
www.ittakestwo.com

JudiKins
(310) 515-1115
www.judikins.com

Junque
www.junque.net

Just For Fun® Rubber Stamps
(727) 938-9898
www.jffstamps.com

K & Company
(888) 244-2083
www.kandcompany.com

Karen Foster Design™ (wholesale only)
(801) 451-9779
www.karenfosterdesign.com

KI Memories
www.kimemories.com

Lasting Impressions for Paper, Inc.
(801) 298-1979
www.lastingimpressions.com

Leaving Prints™
(801) 426-0636
www.leavingprints.com

Leisure Arts, Inc.
(800) 643-8030
www.leisurearts.com

Li'l Davis Designs
(949) 838-0344
www.lildavisdesigns.com

Liquitex® Artist Materials
(888) 4-ACRYLIC
www.liquitex.com

Magenta Rubber Stamps (wholesale only)
(800) 565-5254
www.magentarubberstamps.com

Making Memories
(800) 286-5263
www.makingmemories.com

Ma Vinci's Reliquary
http://crafts.dm.net/mall/reliquary/

McGill, Inc.
(800) 982-9884
www.mcgillinc.com

me & my BiG ideas® (wholesale only)
(949) 583-2065
www.meandmybigideas.com

Memories Complete™, LLC
(866) 966-6365
www.memoriescomplete.com

Mustard Moon™
(408) 229-8542
www.mustardmoon.com

My Mind's Eye™, Inc.
(801) 298-3709
www.frame-ups.com

NRN Designs
(800) 421-6958
www.nrndesigns.com

Nunn Design
(360) 379-3557
www.nunndesign.com

Offray
www.offray.com

Paper Adventures® (wholesale only)
(800) 727-0699
www.paperadventures.com

Paper Fever, Inc.
(801) 412-0495
www.paperfever.com

Paper Loft, The
(801) 254-1961
www.paperloft.com

Patchwork Paper Design, Inc.
(239) 481-4823
www.patchworkpaper.com

Pebbles, Inc.
(800) 438-8153
www.pebblesinc.com

Plaid Enterprises, Inc.
(800) 842-4197
www.plaidonline.com

Provo Craft® (wholesale only)
(888) 577-3545
www.provocraft.com

Prym-Dritz Corporation
www.dritz.com

PSX Design™
(800) 782-6748
www.psxdesign.com

Punch Bunch, The
(254) 791-4209
www.thepunchbunch.com

QuicKutz®
(888) 702-1146
www.quickutz.com

Ranger Industries, Inc.
(800) 244-211
www.rangerink.com

Rusty Pickle
(801) 272-2280
www.rustypickle.com

Sakura Hobby Craft
(310) 212-7878
www.sakuracraft.com

Scrapbook Wizard™, The
(435) 752-7555
www.scrapbookwizard.com

Scrap Ease®
(800) 272-3874
www.whatsnewltd.com

ScrapSMART
www.scrapsmart.com

ScrapTherapy Designs, Inc.
(800) 333-7880
www.scraptherapy.com

Scrapworks, LLC
(801) 363-1010
www.scrapworks.com

SEI, Inc.
(800) 333-3279
www.shopsei.com

Sizzix
(866) 742-4447
www.sizzix.com

Stamp Craft (see Plaid Enterprises)

Stampabilities®
(800) 888-0321
www.stampabilities.com

Stampendous!®
(800) 869-0474
www.stampendous.com

Stampin' Up!®
(800) 782-6787
www.stampinup.com

Sticker Studio™
(208) 322-2465
www.stickerstudio.com

Treehouse Designs
(877) 372-1109
www.treehouse-designs.com

Trodat® GmbH
www.trodat.net

Tsukineko®, Inc.
(800) 769-6633
www.tsukineko.com

Westrim® Crafts
(800) 727-2727
www.westrimcrafts.com

Wordsworth
(719) 282-3495
www.wordsworthstamps.com

Index